作　　者：黃淑惠
烹飪顧問：李木村
烹　　飪：蘇　宜
設　　計：汪金光・何仲德
　　　　　張方馨・酈慧娟
照　　相：大野現
翻　　譯：史嘉琳
文稿協助：邱澄子・陳素眞・張麗雯
　　　　　賴燕貞・馬優雅・陳常彥
打　　字：東奇照相打字有限公司
　　　　　源豐英文電腦排版社
Author : Huang Su-Huei
Cooking consultant : Lee Mu-Tsun
Dishes prepared by : Su I
Design : Wang Chin-Kuang, He Chung-Teh
　　　　　Fandra Chang, Cynthia Lih
Photography : Aki Ohno
English translation : Karen S. Chung
Collaborators : Cheng-Tzu Chiu, Chen Su-Jen
　　　　　Chang Li-Wen, Lai Yen-Jen
　　　　　Gloria C. Martinez, Chen Chang-Yen

ISBN : 0—941676—16—1

序

從民國六十一年，我選擇了實用的菜餚及點心，編著了「中國菜」及「中國餐點」二書，十多年來廣受讀者的喜愛和讚賞，因此又陸續出版了「中國菜實用專輯」「拼盤與盤飾」以及「海鮮專輯」等三本食譜。為了配合社會的進步和大眾的需要，我將原有的二本食譜「中國菜」及「中國餐點」予以簡單化、效率化，「中國菜」一書已於民國七十三年重新拍照印製以嶄新的面貌出版；而「中國餐點」這本書實際上就是點心與簡餐的綜合體，為了更能專業化和普及化，點心部份，已以「點心專輯」為名，於民國七十四年修訂後出版。

在這繁忙的工業社會每日工作忙碌，為了張羅每天的菜單，深感煩惱，「簡餐專輯」的問世將可對此問題有所幫助。傳統的中國菜，即使是簡樸的家常菜，也多數是準備四菜一湯，顯然繁雜而費時，「簡餐專輯」一書的宗旨是力求精簡，做法簡單，材料容易選購，你只要在食譜中任意挑選一項即夠食用和營養，如想講究些可加上前菜或是湯和點心亦甚方便，以中西合併的方式來搭配烹飪，則效果更盡完美，由於每一個人的喜好和口味不一樣，本書將可幫助大家滿足自己的口慾。

「簡餐專輯」共有四十七道菜餚配有精美圖片和解說，每一道菜餚皆經過多次試作而成，相信能夠使讀者滿意，十多年來感謝讀者給我的鼓勵和支持，使我能在食品藝術中更上層樓，願讀者分享我的喜悅和榮譽。

INTRODUCTION

Since 1972, the practical recipes for Chinese entrees and snacks appearing in Chinese Cuisine and Chinese Snacks have had an ever-increasing and appreciative public following. For this reason, we subsequently published Chinese Cooking for Beginners, Chinese Appetizers and Garnishes, and Chinese Seafood. To serve new reader needs, we then simplified, streamlined, and updated the original Chinese Cuisine and Chinese Snacks cookbooks. The revised edition of Chinese Cuisine came out in 1984 in an eye-catching new format with all new photographs. The original Chinese Snacks volume included a combination of recipes for both snacks and simple meals. The snack portion of this book was edited into a separate volume, also entitled Chinese Snacks, revised edition, and was published in 1985.

Chinese One Dish Meals was designed to help busy people with the day-to-day chore of meal planning. Traditional Chinese cooking, even simple home cooking, usually consists of four entrees plus a soup. This requires a lot more time and effort than most people are willing to invest. It is the goal of Chinese One Dish Meals to offer a selection of delicious yet simple dishes made with ingredients easily available. You need only flip to any page of this book to get an idea for a meal that is both satisfying and nutritious. If you like something a little more elaborate, you may add an appetizer or soup, or even one of the snack recipes. The combination of Chinese cooking and Western serving methods introduced in this book makes the meals especially practical and convenient. Everyone has different tastes and preferences, but this book is certain to have something to please every palate.

This book includes recipes with full color photographs for 47 different dishes. Each recipe has been tested and retested, and we are confident that you will find the dishes both delicious and simple to make. We are very grateful for the encouragement and support we have received from our readers over the past decade and more; it has helped us to constantly improve and innovate. We hope that our readers share, through cooking and eating, the pleasure and honor we feel in presenting these books to you.

黃淑惠

Huang Su Huei

March, 1987

1

目錄 TABLE OF CONTENTS

量器容量參照表 TABLE OF MEASUREMENTS

1 杯（1 飯碗）
1 Cup(1 c.)
236 c.c.

1 大匙（1 湯匙）
1 Tablespoon (1 T.)
15 c.c.

做中國菜、點心必備調味品
SEASONINGS USED TO PREPARE CHINESE FOOD

做菜時常用五味即塩（或醬油）、味精、胡椒、麻油、糖，除此之外，酒、醋、太白粉、炸油，也是厨房不可缺少的必備品。

There are five basic seasonings used in the preparation of Chinese food: salt, soy sauce, pepper, sugar, and sesame oil. Other frequently-used condiments include rice wine or sherry, vinegar, cornstarch, and oil for frying.

Rice wine
Sesame oil
Vinegar
Oil for frying
Cornstarch
Soy sauce
Sugar
Salt
Black pepper

1 小匙（1 茶匙）
1 Teaspoon(1t.)
5 c.c.

做中國菜、點心必備用具
UTENSILS USED TO PREPARE CHINESE FOOD

僅刀、菜板、鍋鏟、漏杓、炒鍋、蒸籠等，數樣用
具，足夠做炒、炸、蒸、燉、燴……等等多種美味
菜餚，唯做點心得另備擀麵桿、篩子、打蛋器等。

Just a few utensils are needed to make most stir-fried,
deep-fried, stewed, and sauce dishes. Some of these
are: a cleaver, a cutting board, a metal spatula, a
strainer, a wok, and a steamer. Some additional utensils,
such as a rolling pin, a sifter, and a wire whisk, are
required to make Chinese-style snacks.

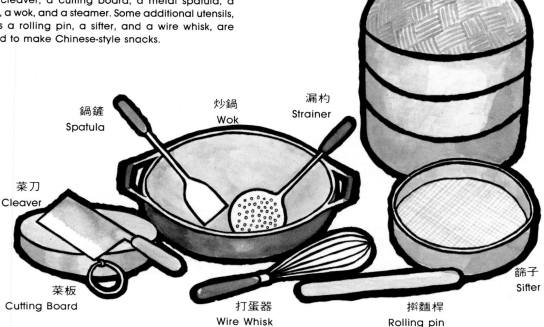

蒸籠
Steamer

鍋鏟
Spatula

炒鍋
Wok

漏杓
Strainer

菜刀
Cleaver

菜板
Cutting Board

打蛋器
Wire Whisk

擀麵桿
Rolling pin

篩子
Sifter

飯與麵的煮法

米 的種類，主要可分爲在萊米與蓬萊米。在萊米形狀長，黏性低。蓬萊米形狀圓，黏性高。如果不喜歡吃太硬或是太軟的飯，可把兩種米混合一起使用之。

煮飯：首先將米搓洗換水多次，以去除雜質和灰塵。瀝乾水份之後，再加入水，米和水的比例１比１。在煮飯之前，如將米浸泡30分鐘以上，則飯更鬆軟、香美。如果時間不允許，不浸泡也可以。

電鍋煮飯：將米洗淨，加入等量的水，浸泡30分鐘以上，蓋上鍋蓋，按下開關煮飯，待開關跳起後再燜約一刻鐘，打開鍋蓋，將飯略鬆鬆即可食用。

普通鍋煮飯：將米洗淨加入等量的水，浸泡30分鐘之後將放米的鍋擱在爐上燒煮，待鍋內水沸騰之後，改小火，繼續煮約20分鐘，燒飯時不可開鍋蓋，熄火後續蓋緊鍋蓋，燜約10分鐘，才可開蓋，將飯翻鬆即可。

麵 的種類很多種，主要可分爲新鮮的濕麵條和乾麵條。也有煮熟的油麵，有普通製和加雞蛋，也有加蔬菜製成的麵條。麵有粗細之分，通常新鮮的濕麵條需冷藏，存放不久，但美味可口。而乾的麵條已除去水份，可保存長久。麵可用來做湯麵、炒麵和燴麵。

煮麵：將鍋內放入大半鍋的水，待水燒開後，放下麵條，煮麵時需要用筷子輕輕攪動，以免麵條黏在一塊。待麵在水中煮開之後，改用小火，以避免沸水溢出。因麵條有乾、濕、粗、細之不同，因而煮麵的時間，需酌量增減，一般而言，中火煮４分鐘即可。如果是做湯麵，將麵條撈起之後，直接放在已調味好的菜湯內即成。如是做炒麵、燴麵，需先將麵條煮熟撈起，用冷水沖涼、瀝乾，拌入少許的食油再使用，冷水沖麵時，時間不可過長，以免麵條過爛。

乾麵一人份的份量爲75公克（２兩）煮後份量約增爲三倍，濕麵一人份的份量爲112.5公克（３兩）煮後份量約增二倍。

HOW TO COOK RICE AND NOODLES

Rice: There are two main types of rice: long grain, which tends to cook up relatively dry; and short grain, which has rounded grains and is stickier when cooked. The two may be combined for rice that is neither too dry nor too sticky.

Electric rice cooker method: Wash the rice, drain, then add water in equal amount to the quantity of rice used. To obtain fluffier rice, the rice may be soaked for 30 minutes or more before cooking; however, this step is optional. Cover and press down the switch. Leave the rice covered for about 15 more minutes after the switch has popped up. Remove the cover and fluff the rice before serving.

Stovetop method: Wash the rice, drain, and add water in equal amount to the quantity of rice used. Soak (optional) for 30 minutes. Cover and bring to a boil over high heat, then lower the heat and let the rice simmer for about 20 minutes. Do not remove the cover during cooking. After turning off the heat, leave the cover on for an additional 10 minutes or so. Remove the cover and fluff the rice before serving.

Noodles: The two main types of noodles are fresh, moist noodles, and dry noodles. There are also precooked noodles (油麵), egg noodles, noodles made with vegetables, broad noodles (much like linguini), and fine noodles (vermicelli). Fresh noodles require refrigeration, and are tastier than dry noodles, but dry noodles can be used just as successfully in the recipes in this book.

Cooking method: Fill a pot a little more than half full with water, bring to a boil, and add the noodles. Separate the noodles with chopsticks to prevent them from sticking together. When the water starts boiling, turn down the heat to medium to prevent the noodles from boiling over. Total cooking time will vary with the type of noodle used; usually four minutes should be enough. For soup noodles, the noodles can go directly into the seasoned broth after cooking. For fried noodles or noodles in sauce, remove the noodles from the cooking water, put into a colander, and run cold water over them. Do not rinse the noodles too long, or they will become mushy. Drain the noodles, then mix in a small amount of cooking oil to prevent them from sticking together. For dry noodles, portion size per person is about 2-1/2 to 3 oz. (75 g.). Volume will be approximately tripled after cooking. For fresh noodles, use about 4 oz. (112.5 g.) per person. Volume will be approximately double after cooking.

肉類基本炒法

在烹飪過程中，炒肉絲、肉片，對於一個初學者，佔了極重要的地位，肉炒出來的嫩、老、是否可口，將影響整個菜餚的好壞。尤其是做中國菜，炒肉絲、肉片的機會很多。一般餐廳的做法是將多量的油加溫，把肉放在油鍋中浸泡，待變色後撈起，再與其他的佐料和配料，混合炒拌，即為一道佳餚。泡過油的肉絲、肉片較鮮嫩，但使用的油量太多，不適合一般家庭使用。本書考慮到主婦操作的方便，特介紹以少量的油，炒肉片、肉絲的方法。

BASIC METHOD FOR STIR-FRYING MEAT

Learning how to properly stir-fry meat shreds and slices is an extremely important part of learning to cook Chinese style. The final results of a dish will depend to a great extent on whether the meat is tender and tasty, particularly since stir-fried meat is so frequently a part of Chinese entrees. The method used in most restaurants is to heat a large amount of oil, then add the meat, letting it soak in the oil just until it changes color. It is then removed from the oil and stir-fried with the other ingredients of the dish. Meat prepared in this way is mouthwateringly tender; however, the large amount of oil required makes this method impractical for home use. The method presented in this book is designed for convenience and ease of home preparation, and uses a minimum of oil.

炒肉或蝦仁時，先調好味，拌入少許油，炒時容易炒開。

For meat or shrimp, first add seasonings to marinate, then add a small amount of oil so the pieces will separate easily during stir-frying.

炒菜鍋，先燒熱後放油。再將鍋輕搖一下，使油均勻遍佈於鍋面。

Heat the wok before adding the oil. Carefully tip the wok from side to side to distribute the oil evenly over the surface.

油熱後把肉放入鍋內，如火候弱，靜待一、二秒。

When the oil is hot (not smoking), put the meat into the wok. If the heat is not high enough, wait another second or two.

讓肉略煎熟，再翻面輕輕炒開，以不超過225公克（6兩）的份量較理想。

Let the meat begin to fry, then gently turn it over with a metal spatula, separating the pieces. Ideally, no more than a half pound (225 g.) of meat should be stir-fried at once.

炒至變色時撈出再與其他佐料配料，混合炒拌，中式炒菜鍋，容量大易翻炒，刷洗方便。

Fry the meat until it just changes color, and remove from the wok. Then combine it with the other seasonings and ingredients, and return to the wok to stir-fry. The large capacity of a Chinese wok makes it easy to turn food, and a wok is also simple to clean.

如使用平底鍋用筷子代替鍋鏟，現市面上流行不黏鍋炒中國菜非常理想。

If you use a regular flat-bottomed frying pan, use chopsticks instead of a metal spatula. Frying pans with a non-stick interior are especially well suited to Chinese cooking.

市面上有切好的牛肉片，宜選帶些肥的比較嫩。如太大，可切二段或三段使用。

Presliced beef may be used for this recipe. Beef with some fat on it will be more tender. If the slices are too large, they may be cut once or twice before use.

可用切好的筍片罐頭。

Canned sliced bamboo shoots may be used.

葱切2吋長，分葱白及葱綠。

Cut the green onion into 2″ sections, separating the white part from the green.

葱爆牛肉飯 2人份

牛肉片	⋯⋯⋯⋯⋯	225公克 (6兩)
①	葱(2吋長) ⋯⋯⋯⋯	2杯
	洋菇 ⋯⋯⋯⋯⋯⋯	1杯
	筍(切薄片) ⋯⋯⋯	½杯
②	醬油 ⋯⋯⋯⋯⋯⋯	3大匙
	糖 ⋯⋯⋯⋯⋯⋯⋯	2小匙
	料酒 ⋯⋯⋯⋯⋯⋯	1大匙
	飯 ⋯⋯⋯⋯⋯⋯⋯	2碗

❶油2大匙燒熱，先將①料內的葱白爆香再入其他各料略炒盛出。

❷油3大匙燒熱，放入牛肉炒至變色，先加②料炒拌，再加炒好的①料翻炒即成。

❸盤內盛飯，上置葱爆牛肉，可與其他蔬菜配食。

BEEF WITH GREEN ONION OVER RICE SERVES 2

①	1/2 lb. (225 g.) beef, sliced
	2 c. green onion, cut in 2″ (5 cm) sections
	1 c. fresh mushrooms
	1/2 c. bamboo shoots, thinly sliced
②	3 T. soy sauce
	2 t. sugar
	1 T. cooking wine or sherry
	2 c. cooked rice

❶ Heat 2 tablespoons oil in a preheated wok. Add the white part of the green onion, fry until fragrant, then add the other ingredients in ①. Stir-fry briefly, then remove from wok.

❷ Heat another 3 tablespoons of oil in the wok, add the beef, and stir-fry until it changes color. Add ②, stir-fry briefly, then add ①, and stir-fry briefly again. Remove from wok.

❸ Put half of the rice onto each of two serving plates, and top with the beef with green onion. Other vegetables may be served as an accompaniment to this dish.

甜麵醬有瓶裝、罐裝，如無則用醬油取代。
Sweet bean paste comes in either jars or cans. If unavailable, use soy sauce as a substitute.

味全京醬可取代②料，味佳且方便。
Wei-Chuan's Peking Sauce may be used as a delicious and convenient substitute for the ingredients in ②.

任何種類之冷凍小粒蔬菜均可用來炒醬味肉末飯。
Any kind of frozen vegetable that comes in small pieces may be used in this recipe.

醬味肉末飯 2人份

絞肉‥‥‥‥‥‥‥‥‥‥225公克 (6兩)
洋蔥(切碎)‥‥‥‥‥‥‥‥‥‥‥½杯
① 熟紅蘿蔔(切丁)‥‥‥‥‥‥ ⎱
  青豆仁‥‥‥‥‥‥‥‥‥‥ ⎰ 共1½杯
  醬油‥‥‥‥‥‥‥‥‥‥‥ 2大匙
② 水、甜麵醬‥‥‥‥‥‥‥‥ 各1大匙
  料酒、糖‥‥‥‥‥‥‥‥‥ 各½大匙
  太白粉、麻油‥‥‥‥‥‥‥ 各1小匙
  飯‥‥‥‥‥‥‥‥‥‥‥‥ 2碗

❶油1大匙燒熱,將①料略炒盛出,再加油3大匙炒香洋蔥,入絞肉炒熟,加②料拌勻,最後放回①料炒勻盛出。
❷盤內盛飯,上置京醬肉末,與蔬菜配食。
■甜麵醬因廠牌不同,其甜度及濃度也不同,故調味料需酌量增減。

GROUND PORK WITH SWEET BEAN PASTE OVER RICE SERVES 2.

1/2 lb. (225 g.) ground pork
1/2 c. onion, chopped
① total of 1-1/2 c.:
  cooked carrot, cut into
    1/2" cubes,
  peas
  2 T. soy sauce
  1 T. each: water,
    sweet bean paste
② 1/2 T. each: cooking wine
    or sherry, sugar
  1 t. each: cornstarch, sesame oil
  2 c. cooked rice

❶ Heat 1 tablespoon oil in a preheated wok. Stir-fry ① briefly and remove from wok. Add 3 more tablespoons of oil to the wok and fry the onion until fragrant. Add the ground pork and stir-fry until cooked through. Add ② and mix in thoroughly. Finally, return ① to the wok, mix in well, and remove from wok.
❷ Put one cup rice on each of two serving plates, and top with the ground pork with sweet bean paste. Other vegetables may be served as an accompaniment to this dish.
■ Because the degree of sweetness and concentration of sweet bean paste varies from brand to brand, the amount used in this recipe may have to be either increased or decreased, according to taste.

魚肉切片。
Cut the fish into slices.

拌好的麵糊，濃稀度如恰當則容易沾，太稀或太濃都不容易沾得住。
The batter should be just the right consistency for best results.

酒釀：糯米飯加糖及酒麴發酵製成，市面上有賣，如無可用酒取代。
Fermented sweet rice is glutinous rice fermented with sugar and yeast, and is sold commercially. If unavailable, wine may be used as a substitute.

茄汁炸魚飯 2人份

	魚肉·······················225公克（6兩）	
①	料酒······························1小匙	
	塩·····························⅓小匙	
	麵粉·····························¼杯	
	麵糊：	
	麵粉、太白粉·················各3大匙	
②	蛋·······························1個	
	水·····························2大匙	
	「炸油」······················適量	
	葱、薑、蒜末·················各1大匙	
	番茄醬·························3大匙	
③	酒釀（或酒）···················1大匙	
	辣豆瓣醬·······················1小匙	
	水·····························1杯	
	糖·····························1大匙	
④	太白粉·······················½大匙	
	塩·····························⅔小匙	
	飯·····························2碗	

❶魚肉切片，加①料拌醃。②料調勻成麵糊。③、④料調好備用。

❷「炸油」燒熱，將魚片沾麵粉再沾麵糊炸至外皮酥且肉熟，撈出。

❸油２大匙燒熱，炒香葱、薑、蒜末，入③料略炒，再加④料炒拌燒開成濃稠狀，離火。即為淋汁。

❹盤內盛飯，上置炸好的魚片，淋上淋汁，以蔬菜配食。

DEEP-FRIED FISH IN TOMATO SAUCE OVER RICE SERVES 2

① 1/2 lb. (225 g.) fish fillet
1 t. cooking wine or sherry
1/3 t. salt
1/4 c. flour

② batter:
3 T. each: flour, cornstarch
1 egg
2 T. water

oil for deep-frying

1 T. each: green onion,
ginger root, garlic; all minced

③ 3 T. ketchup
1 T. fermented sweet rice (酒釀)
or wine
1 t. hot bean paste

④ 1 c. water
1 T. sugar
1/2 T. cornstarch
2/3 t. salt

2 c. cooked rice

❶ Cut the fish in slices and marinate in ①. Mix ② together until thoroughly blended. Mix the ingredients in ③ and ④ separately and set aside.

❷ Heat the oil for deep-frying. Dredge the fish slices in flour, then dip them in the batter. Deep-fry until crispy and golden. Remove from wok.

❸ Heat 2 tablespoons oil in a preheated wok and stir-fry the green onion, ginger, and garlic until fragrant. Add ③, stir-fry briefly, then add ④ and stir-fry until it boils and thickens. Remove from heat. This is the sauce to top the fish.

❹ Put half of the rice on each of two serving plates, arrange the fish on the rice, pour the sauce over the top, and serve with vegetables.

蝦去殼洗淨後使用。
Shell the shrimp and wash before use.

蝦仁可用牙籤挑除沙筋。
Use a toothpick to devein the shrimp.

可用刀，片開取沙筋，如蝦仁比較大也可切爲二半使用。
A razor blade may also be used to devein the shrimp. If the shrimp are large, they may be cut in half lengthwise.

茄汁烹蝦飯 ^{2人份}

蝦仁·····················225公克 (6兩)

① 太白粉····················· 2小匙
料酒························ 1小匙
塩·······················⅓小匙

② 薑、蒜末················· 各1大匙
洋葱 (切碎)················ ½杯

③ 番茄醬···················· 3大匙
酒釀 (或酒)··············· 1大匙
辣豆瓣醬·················· 1小匙

④ 水·······················½杯
太白粉···················· ½大匙
糖·······················⅔大匙
塩·······················½小匙

飯························ 2碗

❶蝦仁加塩1小匙、水1大匙輕輕抓拌,用清水漂洗,瀝乾水份,加①料拌醃。②、③、④料分別調好備用。
❷油3大匙燒熱,將蝦仁炒熟撈出。再加油2大匙,將②料依序放入炒香,隨入③料爆香,加④料攪拌成濃汁,再加入炒好蝦仁即成。
❸盤上盛飯,上置炒好的茄汁蝦仁,與蔬菜配食。
■酒釀:糯米飯加糖及酒麴發酵製成。

SHRIMP IN TOMATO SAUCE OVER RICE SERVES 2

1/2 lb. (225 g.) shelled shrimp

①
2 t. cornstarch
1 t. cooking wine or sherry
1/3 t. salt

②
1 T. each: garlic, ginger root; both minced
1/2 c. onion, diced

③
3 T. ketchup
1 T. fermented sweet rice (酒釀) or wine
1 t. hot bean paste

④
1/2 c. water
1/2 T. cornstarch
2/3 T. sugar
1/2 t. salt

2 c. cooked rice

❶ Add 1 teaspoon salt and 1 tablespoon water to the shrimp and mix gently. Rinse in a colander under running water. Drain, then remove as much moisture from the shrimp as possible with paper towels. Marinate the shrimp in ①. Mix ②, ③, and ④ separately and set aside.
❷ Heat 3 tablespoons oil in a preheated wok. Stir-fry the shrimp until just done, and remove from wok. Add 2 more tablespoons oil to the wok, put the ingredients in ② into the oil, one at a time, and stir-fry until fragrant. Add ③ and stir-fry, then add ④, and stir-fry until thickened. Finally, mix in the cooked shrimp.
❸ Put half of the rice on each of two serving plates, top with the shrimp in tomato sauce, and serve with vegetables.
■ Fermented sweet rice is made from glutinous rice, sugar, and yeast.

乾辣椒因產地不同，其辣度也有輕重之分，炒時需要特別注意，避免用大火以免燒焦。

Dried peppers will have various degrees of piquancy depending on place of origin. Take special care not to use too high heat when stir-frying the peppers or they will burn.

鷄肉面上用刀角略剁容易入味。

Scoring the chicken will help it better absorb the seasonings.

切 1 公分小丁。

Cut the chicken into approx. 1/2″ (1 cm) cubes.

乾椒鷄丁飯 <small>2人份</small>

	鷄肉⋯⋯⋯⋯⋯⋯⋯⋯⋯	225公克（6兩）
①	料酒、醬油⋯⋯⋯⋯⋯⋯	各1大匙
	太白粉⋯⋯⋯⋯⋯⋯⋯⋯	1大匙
	乾辣椒（2公分長）⋯⋯⋯⋯⋯	¼杯
	葱（切粒）⋯⋯⋯⋯⋯⋯⋯	½杯
	水、醬油⋯⋯⋯⋯⋯⋯⋯	各3大匙
	糖⋯⋯⋯⋯⋯⋯⋯⋯⋯⋯	1大匙
②	太白粉⋯⋯⋯⋯⋯⋯⋯⋯	1½小匙
	料酒、醋、麻油⋯⋯⋯⋯	各1小匙
	花生壓碎4大匙或炒香芝麻⋯	2小匙
	飯⋯⋯⋯⋯⋯⋯⋯⋯⋯⋯	2碗

❶鷄肉攤開在肉面上略劃刀，或用刀角略剁（以使入味），切丁，加①料調勻，炒前再拌入1大匙油則肉易炒散開。②料調勻置碗內備用。

❷油３大匙燒熱，先炒乾辣椒，呈褐色隨入鷄肉丁炒至熟，最後加②料用大火迅速炒拌，並加葱粒上撒花生即可。

❸盤內盛飯，上置炒好的乾椒鷄丁，與蔬菜配食。

■如使用味全宮保醬，先將鷄丁或蝦仁炒好，放入醬炒拌均勻即可。

CHICKEN WITH DRIED PEPPERS OVER RICE <small>SERVES 2</small>

	1/2 lb. (225 g.) chicken fillet	
①	1 T. each: cooking wine or sherry, soy sauce	
	1 T. cornstarch	
	1/4 c. dried pepper (3/4" or 2 cm long)	
	1/2 c. chopped green onion	
	3 T. each: water, soy sauce	
	1 T. sugar	
②	1-1/2 t. cornstarch	
	1 t. each: cooking wine or sherry, vinegar, sesame oil	
	4 T. crushed peanuts or 2 t. toasted sesame seeds	
	2 c. cooked rice	

❶ Spread chicken meat open on a cutting board and score with a knife so that it will better absorb the seasonings. Cut into 1/2" cubes and mix in ① to marinate. Mix in 1 tablespoon oil before cooking so that the pieces will separate easily during stir-frying. Mix ② together in a bowl and set aside.

❷ Heat 3 tablespoons cooking oil in a preheated wok. Add the dried peppers and fry until they begin to brown. Add the chicken and stir-fry until thoroughly cooked. Add ② and stir-fry over high heat. Sprinkle chopped green onion and crushed peanuts over the top and remove from heat.

❸ Put half of the rice on each of two serving plates. Top with the chicken with dried peppers, and serve with vegetables.

■ If you use Wei-Chuan's Szechuan Sauce, first stir-fry the chicken cubes (or shelled shrimp) until cooked through, then add the sauce, and stir-fry briefly.

蠔油味鮮美，如無可用醬油代替。
Oyster sauce adds a delicious, rich flavor to this dish, but if it is unavailable, soy sauce may be used as a substitute.

鮮草菇或罐頭草菇均可使用。
Fresh or canned straw mushrooms may be used.

毛菇也有罐頭，用起來方便。
Convenient regular canned mushrooms may also be used.

蠔味牛肉飯 ^{2人份}

	瘦牛肉··················	225公克 (6兩)
①	醬油、料酒··············	各1大匙
	太白粉·················	1大匙
②	葱 (3公分長)·············	6小段
	薑··················	6片
③	水··················	½杯
	蠔油、醬油·············	各1½大匙
	料酒·················	½大匙
	太白粉················	2小匙
	糖··················	2小匙
	麻油、胡椒·············	各少許
④	草菇或毛菇·············	1杯
	青花菜或芥蘭 (煮熟)·········	1杯
	紅蘿蔔 (煮熟)············	12片
	飯··················	2碗

❶牛肉切片，加①料調勻，如太乾加少許水，炒前拌入 1 大匙油則肉易炒開。

❷油 3 大匙燒熱，炒香②料續入肉片炒至七分熟，加③料煮開再拌入④料，全部大火迅速炒勻。

❸盤內盛飯，上置炒好蠔味牛肉即成。

■④料內的材料不限，芹菜、洋葱、青椒、香菇等均可使用。

OYSTER-FLAVORED BEEF OVER RICE SERVES 2

	1/2 lb. (225 g.) lean beef
①	1 T. each: soy sauce, cooking wine or sherry
	1 T. cornstarch
②	1 green onion, cut into 1-1/2" (3 cm) sections
	6 slices ginger root, peeled
③	1/2 c. water
	1-1/2 T. each: oyster sauce, soy sauce
	1/2 T. cooking wine or sherry
	2 t. cornstarch
	2 t. sugar
	few drops sesame oil
	pinch of pepper
④	1 c. mushrooms
	1 c. cut broccoli or Chinese broccoli (芥蘭) (blanch in boiling water until bright green and slightly soft, but crunchy)
	12 slices carrot (blanch in boiling water until slightly soft, but crunchy)
	2 c. cooked rice

❶ Cut the beef into 1″ × 2″ slices. Mix in ① and marinate. If the mixture is too dry, add a small amount of water. Mix in 1 tablespoon oil before stir-frying to help prevent the meat from sticking together.

❷ Heat 3 tablespoons oil in a preheated wok. Fry ② until fragrant and add the meat. Stir-fry until the meat just changes color. Mix in ③ and heat until bubbly, then mix in ④. Stir-fry quickly over high heat, making sure the meat and vegetable are evenly coated with the sauce.

❸ Put half of the rice on each of two serving plates, and spoon the beef-vegetable mixture over the top of each.

■Other vegetables, such as celery, onion, green pepper, dried black mushroom (soaked until soft), etc., may be substituted for those in ④.

牛肉宜選帶些肥的，吃起來比較嫩。
Beef with some fat marbling will be more tender.

在肉面上搥鬆及割刀後再切成塊狀。
Cut the beef into chunks after tenderizing and scoring.

如無荸薺可用洋地瓜取代。
If water chestnuts are unavailable, jicama may be substituted.

香烹牛肉球飯 2人份

	牛肉‧‧‧‧‧‧‧‧‧‧‧‧‧‧‧‧‧‧‧‧‧‧‧‧‧‧‧‧‧‧‧‧	225公克 (6兩)
①	醬油、太白粉‧‧‧‧‧‧‧‧‧‧‧‧‧‧‧‧	各1大匙
	蛋黃‧‧‧‧‧‧‧‧‧‧‧‧‧‧‧‧‧‧‧‧‧‧‧‧‧‧‧‧	1個
	太白粉‧‧‧‧‧‧‧‧‧‧‧‧‧‧‧‧‧‧‧‧‧‧‧‧	4大匙
	「炸油」‧‧‧‧‧‧‧‧‧‧‧‧‧‧‧‧‧‧‧‧‧‧‧‧	適量
②	荸薺‧‧‧‧‧‧‧‧‧‧‧‧‧‧‧‧‧‧‧‧‧‧‧‧‧‧‧‧	
	小黃瓜‧‧‧‧‧‧‧‧‧‧‧‧‧‧‧‧‧‧‧‧‧‧‧‧	計3杯
	紅甜椒‧‧‧‧‧‧‧‧‧‧‧‧‧‧‧‧‧‧‧‧‧‧‧‧	
③	薑、蒜末‧‧‧‧‧‧‧‧‧‧‧‧‧‧‧‧‧‧‧‧	各2小匙
	辣豆瓣醬‧‧‧‧‧‧‧‧‧‧‧‧‧‧‧‧‧‧‧‧	1小匙
④	水‧‧‧‧‧‧‧‧‧‧‧‧‧‧‧‧‧‧‧‧‧‧‧‧‧‧‧‧‧‧‧‧	4大匙
	醬油‧‧‧‧‧‧‧‧‧‧‧‧‧‧‧‧‧‧‧‧‧‧‧‧‧‧	2½大匙
	糖、醋、太白粉‧‧‧‧‧‧‧‧‧	各1小匙
	飯‧‧‧‧‧‧‧‧‧‧‧‧‧‧‧‧‧‧‧‧‧‧‧‧‧‧‧‧‧‧‧‧	2碗

❶牛肉搥鬆並在肉面上劃刀後切成塊狀（使容易入味，且炸好的牛肉感覺鬆嫩）拌入①料，炸時沾太白粉，②、③、④料分別備用。

❷「炸油」燒熱，將肉塊以中火炸約4分鐘，至表面酥脆撈出。

❸油2大匙燒熱，將②料略炒盛出，炒時如太乾加少許水，油1大匙，炒③料，再加④料燒開，放入炸好的牛肉及炒好的②料拌均勻即可。

❹盤內盛飯，上置做好的牛肉球即可食。

■②料內的配料，洋蔥、青椒、紅蘿蔔、蘆筍等都可取代。

SAVORY BEEF BALLS OVER RICE SERVES 2

1/2 lb. (225 g.) beef
① 1 T. each: soy sauce, cornstarch
1 egg yolk
4 T. cornstarch
oil for deep-frying
② total of 3 c.:
water chestnuts,
gherkin cucumbers,
sweet red peppers;
uniformly sliced
③ 2 t. each: ginger root, garlic;
both minced
1 t. hot bean paste
④ 4 T. water
2-1/2 T. soy sauce
1 t. each: sugar, vinegar,
cornstarch
2 c. cooked rice

❶ Tenderize the beef by striking it with a meat mallet or the dull edge of a cleaver. Score the meat to help it better absorb the seasonings and to further tenderize it. Cut into chunks. Marinate in ①. Dredge in cornstarch just before deep-frying. Mix ②, ③, and ④ separately and set aside.

❷ Heat the oil for deep-frying. Deep-fry the beef chunks over medium heat for about 4 minutes. Remove from the oil when the surface of the beef is crisp. Remove the oil from the wok.

❸ Heat 2 tablespoons oil. Add ② and stir-fry briefly. If too dry, add a small amount of water. Remove from wok. Heat 1 tablespoon oil, and stir-fry ③ in it briefly. Add ④, mix, and bring to a boil. Add the beef and ②, and mix together well. Remove from heat.

❹ Put half of the rice on each of two serving plates, and top with the savory beef balls. Serve.

■ Onions, green peppers, carrots, bamboo shoots, etc., may be substituted for the ingredients in ②.

豆豉有乾的、濕的，種類很多，均可使用。
Fermented black beans may be dry or moist. Any type may be used in this recipe.

市面上有磨原豉醬即豆豉磨成醬。
Black bean sauce is commercially available. This is simply fermented black beans ground into sauce.

味全豉椒汁即②料及③料的混合製品。
Wei-Chuan's Cantonese Sauce is a combination of the ingredients in ② and ③.

豉汁鷄腿飯 ^{2人份}

鷄腿‧‧‧‧‧‧‧‧‧‧‧450公克（12兩）約2隻

① 料酒‧‧‧‧‧‧‧‧‧‧‧‧‧‧‧‧‧‧‧‧‧1大匙
   塩‧‧‧‧‧‧‧‧‧‧‧‧‧‧‧‧‧‧‧‧‧½小匙
   胡椒‧‧‧‧‧‧‧‧‧‧‧‧‧‧‧‧‧‧¼小匙

② 豆豉（剁碎）‧‧‧‧‧‧‧‧‧‧‧2小匙
   葱、薑、蒜末‧‧‧‧‧‧‧各1小匙

③ 水‧‧‧‧‧‧‧‧‧‧‧‧‧‧‧‧‧‧‧‧‧‧‧‧½杯
   醬油‧‧‧‧‧‧‧‧‧‧‧‧‧‧‧‧‧‧2小匙
   糖‧‧‧‧‧‧‧‧‧‧‧‧‧‧‧‧‧‧‧‧‧½小匙
   胡椒‧‧‧‧‧‧‧‧‧‧‧‧‧‧‧‧‧‧‧少許
   太白粉‧‧‧‧‧‧‧‧‧‧‧‧‧‧‧½大匙
   飯‧‧‧‧‧‧‧‧‧‧‧‧‧‧‧‧‧‧‧‧‧2碗

❶鷄腿在肉面上劃刀（容易入味），拌入①料醃30分鐘以上，烤盤內置鋁箔紙，鷄腿置上，以450°烤40分鐘，烤的中途如覺外皮太焦，得把火力關小，如用蒸的，大火蒸30分鐘即可。
❷油1½大匙，炒香②料，隨入③料煮開成濃稠狀，即成「淋汁」。
❸盤內盛飯，上置鷄腿，澆上淋汁，與蔬菜配食。
■②料的淋汁可用味全豉椒汁，酌加鷄湯烹製。
■鷄腿洗淨後得擦乾水份使用。
■烤或蒸餘汁可加在③料內，但水及醬油需減少，做好的淋汁可用來炒肉或蝦，味道鮮美，如無豆豉可用醬油取代，但豆豉味較香醇。

CHICKEN WITH BLACK BEAN SAUCE OVER RICE SERVES 2

1 lb. (450 g.) chicken legs, about 2

① 1 T. cooking wine or sherry
   1/2 t. salt
   1/4 t. pepper

② 2 t. fermented black beans, finely chopped
   1 t. each: green onion, ginger root, garlic; all minced

③ 1/2 c. water
   2 t. soy sauce
   1/2 t. sugar
   pinch of pepper
   1/2 T. cornstarch
   2 c. cooked rice

❶ Score the chicken legs to help them better absorb the seasonings. Marinate in ① for about 30 minutes or more. Line a baking pan with aluminum foil, place the chicken legs inside, and bake at 450°F for about 40 minutes. If the skin seems to be browning too quickly, lower the heat. The chicken may also be steamed over high heat for about 30 minutes instead of baked.
❷ Heat 1-1/2 tablespoons oil in a preheated wok, and stir-fry ② until fragrant. Add ③ and bring to a boil, forming a thick sauce.
❸ Put half of the rice on each of two serving plates. Place one chicken leg on top of each, then drizzle the sauce over the chicken. Serve with vegetables.
■ Wei-Chuan's Cantonese Sauce plus a little chicken stock may be used as a substitute for the sauce in step ❷.
■ Wash and dry the chicken legs thoroughly before use.
■ The juices released during baking or steaming may be added to ③, but reduce the amount of water and soy sauce used. The sauce used in this recipe (step ❷) is also delicious for stir-fried pork slices or shrimp. If fermented black beans are unavailable, soy sauce may be substituted, but the black beans have a fuller and richer flavor.

味全滷汁只要與水調和即可使用。
Wei-Chuan's Stewing Sauce and water are the only seasonings needed for a simplified version of this recipe.

乾海帶需泡水2小時以上，浸泡時經常換水去黏液，乾海帶37.5公克（1兩）泡過水後增加五倍即180公克（5兩）

Dried seaweed must be soaked 2 hours or more before use. Change the soak water often to rinse away the sticky substance. 1-1/4 oz. (37.5 g.) of dry seaweed will increase to about 5 times its original weight, about 6-1/4 oz. (180 g.)

豆腐脱水即成豆腐乾，市面上有黃、白、褐色等不同種類，均可使用。

Pressed bean curd is simply bean curd with some of the water removed. Any of the various types available — tan, white, or brown — may be used in this recipe.

滷味飯 6人份

	牛腱子	900公克 (1½斤)
	醬油	½杯
	水	3杯
①	料酒	2大匙
	冰糖	1大匙
	葱	2枝
	薑	4片
	豆腐干	1包4塊
	海帶	37.5公克 (1兩)
	鷄蛋	6個
	飯	6碗

❶將牛腱整個或切半在滾水內川燙撈出。放入①料內，小火燒煮約2小時，至筷子能插入牛肉即可撈出。餘汁可分別滷豆腐干(10分鐘)海帶(20分鐘)鷄蛋(30分鐘)，鷄蛋滷過後浸泡在滷汁內隔夜更好吃。爲節省時間，可將牛腱滷到1小時後，將各料分別放入與牛腱一起滷。

❷盤內盛飯，將材料切好，擺在飯上，澆上滷汁即可。

■除滷牛腱子、豆腐干、海帶、鷄蛋外，鷄、鴨、豬蹄蹄、內臟等均爲滷味的好材料。

SOY-STEWED BEEF OVER RICE SERVES 6

① 2 lb. (900 g.) beef shank
1/2 c. soy sauce
3 c. water
2 T. cooking wine or sherry
1 T. rock sugar
2 green onions
4 slices ginger root
1 package (4 cakes) pressed bean curd (豆腐干)
1-1/4 oz. (37.5 g.) seaweed (kelp)
6 hard-boiled eggs, shelled
6 c. cooked rice

❶ Cut the beef shank in half. Blanch in boiling water and remove. Put into a pot with ①. Stew over low heat for about 2 hours, until a chopstick can easily penetrate the meat. Remove the meat from the pot. Cook the pressed bean curd (for 10 minutes), the seaweed (20 minutes), and the hard-boiled eggs (30 minutes) in the liquid left from cooking the beef. After the eggs have been cooked in the liquid, leave them in the liquid; they will taste even better the next day. To reduce cooking time, the pressed bean curd, seaweed, and hard-boiled eggs may be added to cook with the beef according to the cooking time required, after the beef shank has stewed for one hour.

❷ Put one cup of rice on each of six serving plates. Slice the beef, the pressed bean curd, the seaweed, and the eggs, and arrange on the rice. Pour some of the liquid over the top of each, and serve.

■In addition to beef shank, pressed bean curd, seaweed, and hard-boiled eggs, chicken, duck, pork shoulder, and internal organs may also be prepared in this way.

牛腩參雜些肥肉比較好吃。牛筋不易煮熟，需煮2小時以上。
Fat-marbled beef will be more tender. Beef sinews are tough and require at least two hours of cooking time.

白蘿蔔切塊。
Cut the white radish into 1" cubes.

紅蘿蔔切塊。
Cut the carrots into 1" cubes.

紅燒牛腩飯 6人份

①	牛腩、牛筋⋯⋯ 各450公克 (12兩)
	醬油⋯⋯⋯⋯⋯⋯⋯⋯⋯⋯½杯
	料酒⋯⋯⋯⋯⋯⋯⋯⋯⋯⋯2大匙
	葱⋯⋯⋯⋯⋯⋯⋯⋯⋯⋯⋯2枝
	薑⋯⋯⋯⋯⋯⋯⋯⋯⋯⋯⋯2片
	水⋯⋯⋯⋯⋯⋯⋯⋯⋯⋯⋯4杯
	糖⋯⋯⋯⋯⋯⋯⋯⋯⋯⋯⋯1大匙
②	白蘿蔔(切塊)⋯⋯⋯⋯⋯⋯3杯
	紅蘿蔔(切塊)⋯⋯⋯⋯⋯⋯1杯
	飯⋯⋯⋯⋯⋯⋯⋯⋯⋯⋯⋯6碗

❶將牛腩牛筋放入滾水內川燙撈出，牛筋盛於鍋內，加①料燒開，小火燒煮2小時，續入牛肉再煮1小時至肉熟軟，汁剩約1½杯。

❷白蘿蔔、紅蘿蔔煮熟，放入紅燒牛肉內，燒煮約5分鐘熄火。

❸盤內盛飯，上置燒好的紅燒牛肉與蔬菜配食。

BEEF TENDERLOIN IN SOY SAUCE OVER RICE SERVES 6

1 lb. (450 g.) each:
beef tenderloin, beef sinews

① 1/2 c. soy sauce
2 T. cooking wine or sherry
2 green onions
2 slices ginger root
4 c. water
1 T. sugar

② 3 c. white radish (daikon), cut in 1" (2.5 cm) cubes
1 c. carrots, cut in 1" (2.5 cm) cubes

6 c. cooked rice

❶ Blanch the beef tenderloin and beef sinews in boiling water and remove. Put the beef sinews in a pot with ①. Bring to a boil, then simmer over low heat for 2 hours. Add the beef tenderloin and cook for another hour, until about 1-1/2 cups of liquid remain.

❷ Cook the white radish and carrot until soft, then add to the beef. Cook about 5 minutes, then turn off the heat.

❸ Put one cup of rice on each of 6 serving plates. Top with the beef, and serve with vegetables.

將肉調①料仔細攪拌均勻，分成4
或6個肉丸。
Mix ① carefully into the ground
pork and form into 4 or 6 meatballs.

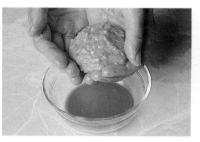

每個肉丸四面沾上調好的②料，略
按扁再放入鍋內煎。
Dip all sides of the meatballs in
②, flatten them a bit, then pan-fry.

蒸丸子時用電鍋或蒸鍋均可，蒸時
外鍋內放水4杯燒開，鍋底墊高，
再把備好的丸子置上，蓋鍋蒸30分。
Use an electric rice cooker or
steamer to steam the meatballs.
Bring 4 cups water to a boil in
the steamer, place an object on
the bottom to hold the plate, and
steam the meatballs for 30 minutes.

豆腐丸子飯 ^{2人份}

絞肉 · · · · · · · · · · · · · · · · · · 225公克 (6兩)
蛋 (小) · 1個
豆腐壓碎¼杯或水 · · · · · · · · · · 2大匙
① 太白粉、料酒 · · · · · · · · · · · · 各½大匙
葱、薑末 · · · · · · · · · · · · · · · 各1小匙
塩 · ½小匙
麻油、胡椒 · · · · · · · · · · · · · · 各少許
② 醬油、水 · · · · · · · · · } 各½大匙，調勻
太白粉 · · · · · · · · · · ·
水 · ½杯
③ 醬油 · 1大匙
糖 · 1小匙
④ 水 · 1大匙
太白粉 · ½大匙
飯 · 2碗

❶絞肉加①料仔細拌勻，做成6個扁肉丸子。
❷油4大匙燒熱，將丸子邊逐個沾上②料邊放入鍋內，煎呈金黃色，移入容器內，加③料蒸30分鐘取出。
❸盤內盛飯，上置肉丸。蒸丸子餘汁燒沸，加④料勾芡成薄汁，淋在肉丸及飯上，與蔬菜配食。
■絞肉內加豆腐或水，燒出來的肉丸，吃起來滑嫩，也可將土司浸在水內，擠乾後放入使用。

BEAN CURD AND PORK BALLS OVER RICE SERVES 2

1/2 lb. (225 g.) ground pork
1 small egg
1/4 c. bean curd, mashed or
  2 T. water
1/2 T. each: cornstarch,
  cooking wine or sherry
① 1 t. each: green onion,
  ginger root; both finely minced
1/2 t. salt
few drops sesame oil
pinch of pepper
② 1/2 T. each, mixed together:
  soy sauce, water, cornstarch
1/2 c. water
③ 1 T. soy sauce
1 t. sugar
④ 1 T. water
1/2 T. cornstarch
2 c. cooked rice

❶ Carefully mix ① into the ground pork, and form into 6 flat meatballs.
❷ Heat 4 tablespoons oil in a preheated wok. Dip the meatballs in ② and fry in the oil until golden. Remove and place in a deep dish with ③. Steam 30 minutes and remove.
❸ Put one cup rice on each of two serving plates, and top with the meatballs. Heat the liquid produced during the steaming and add ④ to thicken slightly. Pour over the meatballs and rice, and serve with vegetables.
■Meatballs made with bean curd or water are especially light and tender. White bread may also be soaked in water, squeezed dry, and added to the ground pork.

在市場買來剁好的豬蹄用起來方便。
Buy pre-cut pigsfeet for extra
convenience.

用冰糖燒煮出來的肉不但顏色好看
且好吃。
Rock sugar lends a beautiful color
and delicious flavor to this dish.

肉內加一朵八角紅燒，增加香味。
Star anise adds extra flavor.

紅燒蹄飯 3－4人份

	前腿蹄	1200公克 (2斤)
	醬油	1½ 大匙
	葱段 (2.5公分長)	6段
	蒜瓣	4粒
①	水	3杯
	醬油	¾ 杯
	料酒	1大匙
	冰糖 (或糖)	½ 大匙
	八角 1朵 (或五香粉¼小匙)	
	飯	4碗

❶豬蹄如有毛或垢穢應用刀刮除乾淨，剁成5—6塊，放入開水內川燙撈出，瀝乾水份抹上醬油備用。

❷油４大匙燒熱，把葱、蒜炒香，放入豬蹄將外皮煎炒至金黃色後，加①料以中火燒煮40分鐘，用筷子插入試試是否軟了，煮至汁剩1½杯即可離火。

❸盤內盛飯，上置豬蹄，淋上餘汁，與蔬菜配食。

■此道飯點做法及材料均簡單，又可口，是一道理想的簡餐。唯豬蹄一定要燒煮至汁剩1½杯，味道才够濃。

PIGSFEET IN SOY SAUCE OVER RICE SERVES 3-4

- 2-2/3 lb. (1,200 g.) pigsfeet (fore feet)
- 1-1/2 T. soy sauce
- 6 1" (2.5 cm) sections of green onion
- 4 cloves garlic, peeled
- ① 3 c. water
- 3/4 c. soy sauce
- 1 T. cooking wine or sherry
- 1/2 T. rock sugar or white sugar
- 1 floweret star anise (or 1/4 t. five-spice powder)
- 4 c. cooked rice

❶ Use a knife to scrape off any hairs or foreign material from the pigsfeet. Chop into 5 to 6 pieces. Blanch in boiling water. Remove, drain, and spoon the soy sauce over the outer surface of the pigsfeet. Set aside.

❷ Heat 4 tablespoons oil in a preheated wok. Fry the green onion and garlic until fragrant. Put in the pigsfeet and fry until the surface is golden brown. Add ① and cook over medium heat for 40 minutes. Cook until about 1-1/2 cups liquid remain, and a chopstick inserted into the meat penetrates it easily. Remove from heat.

❸ Put the rice on serving plates, place the pigsfeet over the rice, and pour some of the liquid over the top of each. Serve with vegetables.

■ This delicious dish is uncomplicated in method and materials, so it is ideal for a quick, simple meal. Just make sure about 1-1/2 cups of liquid remain at the end of the cooking to ensure a rich flavor.

豬肉排或牛肉排均可。
Either pork or beef cutlets can be used in this recipe.

市面上有切好一片一片的火鷄胸肉，用起來非常方便。
Convenient, ready-cut turkey breast fillets may also be used in this recipe.

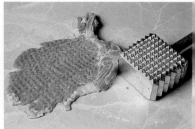

肉排事先用刀捶鬆，肉邊的筋略切，以免收縮。
Use the dull edge of a cleaver to tenderize the cutlets. Some of the sinews on the outer edges may be cut to prevent shrinking.

茄汁肉排飯 2人份

	豬肉排2片 …………	337.5公克(9兩)
①	醬油、太白粉 …………	各1大匙
	料酒 …………………	1大匙
②	洋葱(切絲) …………	1杯
	辣椒(切絲) …………	2大匙
③	水 ……………………	½杯
	醬油 …………………	3大匙
	糖、醋、番茄醬 ………	各1½大匙
	太白粉 ………………	½大匙
	飯 ……………………	2碗

❶肉排用刀背或捶肉器捶鬆，加①料調勻。

❷油2大匙燒熱，將肉排兩面煎呈金黃色(每面約煎1分半鐘)且肉熟鏟出。另加油1大匙，將②料炒香，再入③料燒開，放回肉排炒拌均勻即成。

❸盤內盛飯，上置煮好的茄汁肉排，與蔬菜配食。

PORK CUTLET IN TOMATO SAUCE OVER RICE SERVES 2

	2 pork cutlets (3/4 lb. or 337.5 g.)
①	1 T. each: soy sauce, cornstarch
	1 T. cooking wine or sherry
②	1 c. onion, cut in thin half rings
	2 T. hot red peppers, finely shredded
③	1/2 c. water
	3 T. soy sauce
	1-1/2 T. each: sugar, vinegar, ketchup
	1/2 T. cornstarch
	2 c. cooked rice

❶ Pound the pork cutlet with the dull edge of a cleaver or a meat mallet to tenderize. Mix in ① to coat evenly.

❷ Heat 2 tablespoons oil in a preheated wok. Fry the pork cutlets on both sides until cooked through and golden brown, about 1-1/2 minutes per side. Remove from wok. Add one more tablespoon oil to the wok. Fry ② until fragrant, then add ③ and heat until bubbly. Return the cutlet to the wok, and turn over a few times in the sauce. Remove from heat.

❸ Put one cup of rice on each of two serving plates, and place one pork cutlet in tomato sauce on top of each. Serve with vegetables.

除將炒好的料澆在飯上食用外，市
面上賣各種不同麵皮（如圖1.2.3.）
或春捲皮、荷葉餅等均可塗上海鮮
醬包捲而食。

As an alternative to serving over
rice, spread some hoisin sauce
(sweet bean paste) on a Moo Shu
shell (like those used for Peking
Duck; commercially available),
and wrap around the stir-fried
mixture. (See illustrations 1, 2, 3.)

蛋肉菠菜飯 2人份

	瘦肉(豬、牛或雞)···150公克(4兩)	
①	醬油·············	2小匙
	料酒、太白粉··········	各½大匙
	鶏蛋·············	2個
	菠菜·············	225公克(6兩)
②	洋葱(切片)·········	
	洋菇(切片)·········	3杯
	番茄或紅蘿蔔(切片)·······	
③	水··············	4大匙
	塩··············	¾小匙
	糖··············	1小匙
	太白粉············	1小匙
	胡椒、麻油··········	各少許
	飯··············	2碗

❶將肉切片，加①料調勻。蛋打散，菠菜洗淨略切，②、③料備用。

❷油1大匙燒熱，將蛋炒至凝固鏟出，油各1大匙燒熱，把菠菜及肉片分別略炒鏟出，再加油2大匙炒②料，放回肉、鶏蛋、菠菜，再加③料全部大火迅速炒勻即可。

❸盤內盛飯，上置炒好的料即成。

EGG, PORK AND SPINACH OVER RICE SERVES 2

	1/3 lb. (150 g.) lean pork, beef, or chicken	
①	2 t. soy sauce	
	1/2 T. each: cooking wine or sherry, cornstarch	
	2 eggs	
	1/2 lb. (225 g.) spinach	
②	total of 3 c.: onion, sliced fresh mushrooms, sliced tomatoes or carrots, sliced	
③	4 T. water 3/4 t. salt 1 t. sugar 1 t. cornstarch few drops sesame oil pinch of pepper	
	2 c. cooked rice	

❶ Cut the meat into 1"×2" slices. Mix in ① and marinate. Beat the eggs lightly. Wash the spinach thoroughly and cut. Mix ② and ③ separately and set aside.

❷ Heat 1 tablespoon oil in a preheated wok. Stir-fry the egg in the oil until set and remove from wok. Heat another tablespoon of oil in the wok. Stir-fry the spinach in it and remove. Heat yet another tablespoon of oil and stir-fry the meat slices, and remove. Heat 2 tablespoons of oil, and stir-fry ②. When almost done, return the meat, egg, and spinach to the wok with ②. Add ③ and stir-fry quickly over high heat. Remove from heat.

❸ Put half of the rice on each of two serving plates, and top with the stir-fried mixture. Serve.

榨菜：芥葉莖加塩、香料、辣椒粉
醃漬製成，使用時洗去塩份切絲，
泡約10分鐘去鹹份再使用。
Szechuan pickled mustard greens are
stems of mustard greens cured in salt,
spices, and hot red pepper. Wash
before use to remove some of the
saltiness, then shred. Soak about 10
minutes before use to further reduce
the saltiness.

任何種類豆腐干均可使用。
Any type of pressed bean curd
may be used.

有現成的罐頭筍絲用起來方便。
Use canned bamboo shoots for
extra convenience.

豆乾肉絲飯 2人份

①	瘦肉（豬、牛或鷄）‥‥‥225公克（6兩）
	醬油、料酒‥‥‥‥‥‥‥‥各1大匙
	太白粉‥‥‥‥‥‥‥‥‥‥‥1大匙
	葱、薑絲‥‥‥‥‥‥‥‥‥各1大匙
②	筍（切絲）‥‥‥‥‥‥‥‥‥‥1杯
	榨菜（切絲）‥‥‥‥‥‥‥‥‥½杯
	五香豆乾（切絲）‥‥‥‥‥‥‥2塊
	水‥‥‥‥‥‥‥‥‥‥‥‥‥1大匙
③	糖‥‥‥‥‥‥‥‥‥‥‥‥‥1小匙
	塩‥‥‥‥‥‥‥‥‥‥‥‥‥⅛小匙
	麻油、胡椒‥‥‥‥‥‥‥‥各少許
	飯‥‥‥‥‥‥‥‥‥‥‥‥‥2碗

❶肉絲加①料拌勻，炒前再拌入1大匙油，則炒時肉絲易鏟開。
❷油3大匙燒熱，將肉絲放入炒熟盛出，再加油2大匙，將葱、薑炒香，放入②料略炒，隨即加入③料及肉絲，大火炒拌均勻即成。如有青葱段灑上顏色更佳。
❸盤內盛飯，上置炒好的豆乾肉絲即成。

PRESSED BEAN CURD WITH MEAT SHREDS OVER RICE SERVES 2

①	1/2 lb. (225 g.) lean pork, beef, or chicken, cut in fine strips
	1 T. each: soy sauce, cooking wine or sherry
	1 T. cornstarch
	1 T. each: green onion, ginger root; both finely shredded
②	1 c. bamboo shoots, cut in julienne strips
	1/2 c. Szechuan pickled mustard greens, cut in julienne strips
	2 cakes five-spice flavored pressed bean curd, cut in julienne strips
	1 T. water
③	1 t. sugar
	1/8 t. salt
	few drops sesame oil
	pinch of pepper
	2 c. cooked rice

❶ Mix ① into the meat shreds. Mix in 1 tablespoon oil before stir-frying so that the shreds will separate easily when cooking.

❷ Heat 3 tablespoons oil in a preheated wok. Stir-fry the meat shreds in the oil until done. Remove. Heat another 2 tablespoons oil and stir-fry the green onion and ginger root until fragrant, then add ② and stir-fry briefly. Add ③ and the meat shreds and stir-fry quickly over high heat. Make sure all the ingredients are evenly coated with the sauce. A little chopped green onion may be sprinkled on the top.

❸ Put half of the rice on each of two serving plates, and top with the stir-fried mixture. Serve.

乾香菇。
Dried Chinese black mushrooms.

香菇使用時得先泡水，切去蒂後使
用，因香菇的新舊乾濕度不同，泡
水的時間也不定，一般約需20分鐘。
Dried Chinese black mushrooms must
be soaked before use. Cut off and
discard the stems. Soaking time required
will depend on the age and degree
of dryness of the mushrooms. Usually
20 minutes is enough.

筍的種類很多，買罐頭的使用起來
方便，如用新鮮筍宜煮熟後使用。
There are many different types of
bamboo shoots. Canned bamboo
shoots are especially convenient.
Fresh bamboo shoots must be
boiled until soft before use.

蝦仁肉片飯 ^{2人份}

	蝦仁⋯⋯⋯⋯⋯⋯	150公克 (4兩)
①	塩⋯⋯⋯⋯⋯⋯⋯	¼小匙
	料酒⋯⋯⋯⋯⋯⋯	⅔小匙
	太白粉⋯⋯⋯⋯⋯	½大匙
	瘦肉(豬、牛或鷄)⋯	75公克 (2兩)
②	醬油⋯⋯⋯⋯⋯⋯	1小匙
	料酒⋯⋯⋯⋯⋯⋯	½小匙
	太白粉⋯⋯⋯⋯⋯	1小匙
	葱(1吋長)⋯⋯⋯⋯	8枝
③	紅辣椒(切絲)⋯⋯⋯	1大匙
	香菇(切絲)⋯⋯⋯⋯	3朶
④	幼筍或其他筍(切1吋長)⋯	1杯
	荷蘭豆或芹菜⋯⋯⋯	12片
	塩⋯⋯⋯⋯⋯⋯⋯	½小匙
	糖⋯⋯⋯⋯⋯⋯⋯	1小匙
⑤	胡椒⋯⋯⋯⋯⋯⋯	少許
	水⋯⋯⋯⋯⋯⋯⋯	4大匙
	太白粉⋯⋯⋯⋯⋯	1小匙
	飯⋯⋯⋯⋯⋯⋯⋯	2碗

❶蝦仁挑除沙筋,加塩1小匙、水1大匙,輕輕抓拌,用清水漂洗瀝乾水份,加①料拌醃,肉切片加②料調拌。

❷油3大匙燒熱,將蝦仁及瘦肉放入鍋內炒熟撈出。鍋再加油2大匙,先將③料炒香再入④料略炒,再把⑤料及肉、蝦一起放入,大火迅速炒拌即成。

❸盤內盛飯,上置炒好的蝦、肉與蔬菜配食。

SHRIMP WITH MEAT SLICES OVER RICE SERVES 2

	1/3 lb. (150 g.) shrimp, shelled	
①	1/4 t. salt	
	2/3 t. cooking wine or sherry	
	1/2 T. cornstarch	
	2.6 oz. (75 g.) lean pork, beef, or chicken	
②	1 t. soy sauce	
	1/2 t. cooking wine or sherry	
	1 t. cornstarch	
③	8 1" sections of green onion	
	1 T. hot red pepper, shredded	
	3 dried Chinese black mushrooms, soaked and cut in julienne strips	
④	1 c. young bamboo shoots, cut into 1" (2.5 cm) pieces	
	12 snow peas (Chinese peapods) or 12 slices celery	
	1/2 t. salt	
	1 t. sugar	
⑤	pinch of pepper	
	4 T. water	
	1 t. cornstarch	
	2 c. cooked rice	

❶ Devein the shrimp. Gently mix in 1 teaspoon salt and 1 tablespoon water, then rinse under cold water. Drain and pat dry with paper towels. Mix in ①. Cut the meat into slices and marinate in ②.

❷ Heat 3 tablespoons of oil in a preheated wok. Stir-fry the shrimp and meat slices in the oil until cooked through. Remove. Add another 2 tablespoons oil to the wok. Stir-fry ③ until fragrant, then add ④ and continue to stir-fry. Finally, add ⑤ and the meat and shrimp. Stir-fry quickly over high heat. Remove from heat.

❸ Put half of the rice on each of two serving plates, and top with the stir-fried mixture. Serve with vegetables.

青椒切塊。
Cut the green pepper into pieces.

番茄切塊。
Cut the tomato into chunks.

洋蔥切塊。
Cut the onion into chunks.

番茄燴飯 2人份

牛、豬或鷄肉(切片)225公克(6兩)

① 太白粉、水、醬油……… 各1大匙
料酒……………………………½大匙

青椒(切塊)…………………… 1杯

② 洋葱(切塊)
番茄(切塊)
洋菇或草菇 …… 共2杯

③ 水………………………………1杯
番茄醬……………………… 2大匙
糖…………………………… 1大匙
塩………………………………½小匙
胡椒…………………………… 少許
太白粉……………………… 1大匙

飯………………………………2碗

❶肉片加①料拌醃，③料調好備用。
❷油1大匙燒熱，將青椒略炒盛出。油2大匙也把肉炒熟盛出。
❸油2大匙燒熱，依序放入②料略炒，入③料燒開後再入肉及青椒，食時澆在蛋炒飯上即成。
■亦可澆在白飯上，但③料調味汁味要加重些。

蛋炒飯做法：
❶飯2碗，加油½大匙、糖½小匙、塩⅓小匙、胡椒少許備用。
❷油1大匙燒熱，將蛋2個打散炒至凝固後鏟至鍋邊，再加少許油炒飯2分鐘，最後加入葱粒及蛋全部炒勻即成。

MEAT IN KETCHUP SAUCE OVER RICE SERVES 2

1/2 lb. (225 g.) beef, pork, or chicken, sliced

① 1 T. each: cornstarch, water, soy sauce
1/2 T. cooking wine or sherry

1 c. green pepper, cut in pieces

② total of 2 c.:
onion, cut in chunks
tomato, cut in chunks
fresh mushrooms or straw mushrooms

③ 1 c. water
2 T. ketchup
1 T. sugar
1/2 t. salt
pinch of pepper
1 T. cornstarch

2 c. cooked rice

❶ Marinate the meat in ①. Mix ③ and set aside.
❷ Heat 1 tablespoon oil in a wok. Fry the green pepper briefly and remove. Heat 2 tablespoons of oil and stir-fry the meat until done. Remove.
❸ Heat 2 tablespoons oil in the wok. Add the ingredients in ② one by one and stir-fry briefly. Add ③ and bring to a boil. Add the meat and green pepper. Spoon over egg fried rice to serve.
■This dish may also be served over white rice, but make the flavor of sauce ③ stronger.

Egg Fried Rice
❶ Add 1/2 tablespoon oil, 1/2 t. sugar, 1/3 t. salt, and a pinch of pepper to 2 c. cooked rice; mix well. Sugar, salt and pepper may be added in step ❷ when frying the rice.
❷ Heat 1 tablespoon oil in a preheated wok. Lightly beat 2 eggs and stir-fry in the oil until set. Remove. Add a small amount of oil to the wok, and stir-fry the cooked rice in it for about 2 minutes. Add some chopped green onion and the egg; mix well. Remove from heat.

配料有雪豆、紅蘿蔔、草菇，或任
意選用其他材料。

Other vegetables may be
substituted for the snow peas,
carrots, and mushrooms.

將拌好的絞肉抓一把在手心，用大
姆指將肉抹平，同時慢慢將手握緊，
丸子就被推擠出來。

Place a small amount of ground
meat in the palm of your hand.
Pat the meat down flat with your
thumb, while at the same time
bringing together a fist around
the meat.

此時將湯匙沾水後，把丸子搯出放
入油內炸（湯匙沾水可避免肉黏在
湯匙上）。

Scoop the meatball out with a
spoon dipped in water. Drop the
meatball into the oil to deep-fry.
(Dipping the spoon in water
prevents the meat from sticking
to the spoon.)

三蔬丸子燴飯 2人份

①	絞肉（豬或牛肉）……225公克（6兩）	
	太白粉、醬油…………… 各1大匙	
	蛋1個或水…………… 2大匙	
	料酒、糖…………… 各½大匙	
	青葱或洋葱（切碎）…… 2大匙	
	麵粉…………… 2大匙	
②	「炸油」……適量	
	雪豆……12片	
	蒜末……½大匙	
	辣椒……適量	
	紅蘿蔔（切滾刀塊）……… } 共3杯	
	草菇或洋菇	
③	水…………… 1杯	
	醬油…………… 1½大匙	
	糖…………… 1小匙	
	塩…………… ⅙小匙	
	胡椒…………… 少許	
	太白粉…………… 1⅓大匙	
	飯…………… 2碗	

❶絞肉加①料拌醃，③料調好備用。

❷「炸油」燒熱，將絞肉擠成丸子（約16個），放入油內炸3分鐘，呈金黃色撈出，油½大匙燒熱，將雪豆加少許水略炒盛出。

❸油2大匙燒熱，放入②料內之蒜末、辣椒爆香，再依序入他料略炒，放入③料及丸子燒開，加雪豆澆在飯上即成。

MEATBALLS WITH VEGETABLES IN SOY SAUCE OVER RICE SERVES 2

① 1/2 lb. (225 g.) ground pork
   or ground beef
1 T. each: cornstarch, soy sauce
1 egg or 2 T. water
1/2 T. each: cooking wine
   or sherry, sugar
2 T. onion or green onion,
   minced
2 T. flour

oil for deep-frying
12 snow peas
   (Chinese peapods)

② 1/2 T. garlic, minced
hot red pepper, as desired
total of 3 c.:
   carrots, roll-cut
   fresh mushrooms
      or straw mushrooms

③ 1 c. water
1-1/2 T. soy sauce
1 t. sugar
1/6 t. salt
pinch of pepper
1-1/3 T. cornstarch
2 c. cooked rice

❶ Mix ① into the ground meat. Mix ③ separately and set aside.

❷ Heat the oil for deep-frying. Form the meat into about 16 meatballs. Deep-fry in the oil until golden brown, about 3 minutes. Remove from oil. Remove oil from wok. Heat 1/2 tablespoon oil and briefly stir-fry the snow peas with a little water. Remove.

❸ Heat 2 tablespoons of oil. Stir-fry the garlic and hot red pepper of ② until fragrant. Then add the other ingredients of ② one by one. Add ③ and the meatballs, and bring to a boil. Add the snow peas. Spoon over rice to serve.

肉切丁拌入①料。
Cut the meat into cubes and add ①

洋芋、紅蘿蔔均切丁。
Cube the potato and carrot.

咖哩粉廠牌不同辣度也不同，依喜好酌加辣椒或辣椒醬。
There are many brands of curry powder available with many different degrees of piquancy. If you like your curry hotter, add a little hot red pepper or chili paste.

咖哩飯 2人份

	雞肉或豬、牛肉（切丁）225公克（6兩）	
①	塩	¼小匙
	料酒、太白粉	各1大匙
	咖哩粉	½大匙
	油	6大匙
②	洋葱丁	½杯
	咖哩粉或油咖哩	3大匙
	麵粉	5大匙
③	洋芋丁	1½杯
	紅蘿蔔丁	1杯
④	雞湯或水	3杯
	塩	1小匙
	糖	½大匙
	胡椒	¼小匙
	料酒	1大匙
	飯	2碗

❶肉丁調①料拌勻備用。

❷油6大匙燒熱，先炒香②料內的洋葱至金黃色，隨入咖哩粉及麵粉略炒，再加③料及④料，煮開後改小火約15分鐘，燒煮時需隨時攪動以免黏鍋，最後加入拌好的肉丁，燒煮數分鐘至熟即成。

CURRY RICE SERVES 2

	1/2 lb. (225 g.) chicken, pork, or beef, cut into cubes
①	1/4 t. salt
	1 T. each: cooking wine or sherry, cornstarch
	1/2 T. curry powder
	6 T. oil
②	1/2 c. onion, cubed
	3 T. curry powder or curry paste
	5 T. flour
③	1-1/2 c. potato, cubed
	1 c. carrot, cubed
④	3 c. chicken stock or water
	1 t. salt
	1/2 T. sugar
	1/4 t. pepper
	1 T. cooking wine or sherry
	2 c. cooked rice

❶ Marinate the meat in ①.

❷ Heat the 6 tablespoons oil in a preheated wok. Fry the onion of ② until fragrant and golden. Add the curry powder and flour and stir-fry briefly. Add ③ and ④; bring to a boil. Simmer over low heat for 15 minutes. Stir frequently while cooking to prevent sticking. Finally, add the meat and cook several minutes until the meat is cooked through.

❸ Put half of the rice on each of two serving plates and top with the curry mixture. Serve.

將材料要沾滿麵糊，太稀太濃都不好沾。
The batter should be neither too thin nor too thick, and should coat the food to be fried completely.

沾滿麵糊後再沾上麵包粉炸，吃起來香脆。
Roll the food in fine bread crumbs after dipping in the batter, then deep-fry. This makes a delicious and crisp outer coating.

沾料無限定，可用現成的。
You may use any dipping sauce of your choice, including commercially prepared ones.

炸蝦蔬菜飯 2人份

<table>
<tr><td rowspan="3">①</td><td>中蝦</td><td>8條</td></tr>
<tr><td>料酒</td><td>½大匙</td></tr>
<tr><td>塩</td><td>⅛小匙</td></tr>
<tr><td></td><td>洋黃瓜</td><td>1條</td></tr>
<tr><td></td><td>茄子</td><td>1條</td></tr>
<tr><td></td><td>四季豆</td><td>8條</td></tr>
<tr><td rowspan="4">②</td><td>冰水</td><td>1杯</td></tr>
<tr><td>蛋</td><td>1個</td></tr>
<tr><td>麵粉</td><td>1杯</td></tr>
<tr><td>發粉</td><td>¼小匙</td></tr>
<tr><td></td><td>麵包粉</td><td>1杯</td></tr>
<tr><td></td><td>「炸油」</td><td>適量</td></tr>
<tr><td></td><td>魚乾汁</td><td>¾杯</td></tr>
<tr><td></td><td>醬油</td><td>2大匙</td></tr>
<tr><td></td><td>糖</td><td>1½小匙</td></tr>
<tr><td></td><td>料酒</td><td>1小匙</td></tr>
<tr><td></td><td>白蘿蔔（磨碎）</td><td>1大匙</td></tr>
<tr><td></td><td>飯</td><td>2碗</td></tr>
</table>

②料 拌勻

沾料

❶蝦去殼留尾，洗淨拭乾水份，由背部片開，去除沙筋再略劃刀，以免炸時翻捲，拌入①料略醃，洋黃瓜、茄子切片。

❷②料內的冰水及蛋先拌，再加拌勻的麵粉，輕輕攪拌成麵糊。

❸「炸油」燒熱，處理好的蝦先沾上麵糊，再沾麵包粉，下鍋炸至表面呈金黃色即可撈出，其他材料做法相同，四季豆可二、三根合起來炸。食時，磨碎白蘿蔔，加入沾料內，將炸好的材料放入沾食。

■魚乾汁做法：小魚乾75公克（2兩）去頭、腸洗淨炒乾，放入水4杯，燒開去泡沫，慢火煮30分鐘，去渣，只要湯汁，做沾料外，也可用來燒湯麵。

■材料種類不限，可隨個人喜愛，就地取材選用魚、肉、馬鈴薯、蕃薯等材料使用。

FRIED SHRIMP WITH VEGETABLES OVER RICE SERVES 2

① 8 medium shrimp
1/2 T. cooking wine or sherry
1/8 t. salt
1 zucchini
1 eggplant
8 string beans

② 1 c. ice water
1 egg
1 c. flour
1/4 t. baking powder
(premix flour and
  baking powder)
1 c. fine bread crumbs
oil for deep-frying
Dipping Sauce:
3/4 c. dried fish broth
2 T. soy sauce
1-1/2 t. sugar
1 t. cooking wine or sherry
1 T. white radish (daikon),
  grated finely
2 c. cooked rice

❶ Shell the shrimp, leaving the tails intact. Wash thoroughly, drain, and pat dry with paper towels. Devein the shrimp. Make a few horizontal cuts on the abdomen of each shrimp to prevent curling. Marinate in ①. Slice the zucchini, and cut the eggplant into slices about the same size as the zucchini slices.

❷ First mix the ice water and egg of ②, then mix in the premixed flour and baking powder to make a batter.

❸ Heat the oil for deep-frying. Dip the prepared shrimp in the batter, then roll in the fine bread crumbs. Deep-fry until golden brown, then remove. Proceed in the same manner to deep-fry the zucchini, eggplant, and string beans. The string beans can be fried in clumps of two or three. When serving, mix the finely grated white radish into the dipping sauce. Dip the fried food in the sauce before eating.

■ To make the dried fish broth: Remove the heads and intestines from 2.6 oz. (75 g.) of small dried fish, and wash. Stir-fry until dry. Add 4 cups of water to the fish. Bring to a boil, and remove the foam that forms. Simmer over low heat for 30 minutes. Strain before use. This broth can also be used to make noodles in broth.

■ Other foods may be used in this recipe, such as fish, meat, potatoes, sweet potatoes, and so forth — whatever is available locally.

豆腐切丁。
Cube the bean curd.

使用冷凍蔬菜，非常簡便。
Use frozen vegetables for extra convenience.

冷凍蔬菜種類不限，可任意選用。
Choose any type of frozen vegetables you like for this recipe.

三色豆腐飯 2人份

牛或豬絞肉‧‧‧‧‧‧‧‧‧‧‧150公克（4兩）
豆腐（切丁）‧‧‧‧‧‧‧‧‧‧‧‧‧‧‧‧‧‧1盒
① 葱（切碎）‧‧‧‧‧‧‧‧‧‧‧‧‧‧‧‧‧2大匙
　 蒜（切碎）‧‧‧‧‧‧‧‧‧‧‧‧‧‧‧‧‧1大匙
　 小紅辣椒（切片）‧‧‧‧‧‧‧‧‧1條
② 醬油‧‧‧‧‧‧‧‧‧‧‧‧‧‧‧‧‧‧‧‧‧‧‧2大匙
　 料酒、糖‧‧‧‧‧‧‧‧‧‧‧‧‧各½大匙
　 塩‧‧‧‧‧‧‧‧‧‧‧‧‧‧‧‧‧‧‧‧‧‧‧½小匙
　 高湯或水‧‧‧‧‧‧‧‧‧‧‧‧‧‧‧‧‧1杯
　 太白粉‧‧‧‧‧‧‧‧‧‧‧‧‧‧‧‧‧‧‧1大匙
③ 青豆仁
　 洋菇
　 紅蘿蔔　　任選一杯
　 玉米粒
　 青葱花‧‧‧‧‧‧‧‧‧‧‧‧‧‧‧‧‧‧‧2大匙
　 飯‧‧‧‧‧‧‧‧‧‧‧‧‧‧‧‧‧‧‧‧‧‧‧2碗

❶油3大匙燒熱，炒香①料放入絞肉炒熟後，加②料及豆腐，待燒開即改小火煮約3分鐘，炒拌成濃稠狀，再加③料燒開，灑上葱花即可。
❷盤內盛飯，上置三色豆腐即可食。

BEAN CURD WITH VEGETABLES OVER RICE SERVES 2

1/3 lb (150 g.) ground beef
　or ground pork
1 large cake bean curd, cubed
① 2 T. green onion, minced
　 1 T. garlic, minced
　 1 hot red pepper, cut in strips
② 2 T. soy sauce
　 1/2 T. each: cooking wine
　　 or sherry, sugar
　 1/2 t. salt
　 1 c. stock or water
　 1 T. cornstarch
③ 1 c. of any one or combination
　　 of the following:
　　 peas, fresh mushrooms,
　　 carrots, whole kernal corn
2 T. green onion, chopped
2 c. cooked rice

❶ Heat 3 tablespoons oil in a preheated wok. Stir-fry ① until fragrant. Add the ground meat and stir-fry until cooked through. Add ② and the bean curd. Bring to a boil, then cook over low heat for 3 minutes. Stir-fry until a thick sauce forms, then add ③. Bring to a boil, then sprinkle the chopped green onion over the top.
❷ Put half of the rice on each of two serving plates, and top with the bean curd and vegetables. Serve.

茄子。
Eggplant.

圓茄子去皮後切條。長茄子不去皮
也可以。

If using large, round eggplant,
peel before using. Long oriental
eggplant need not be peeled.

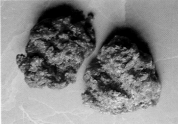

牛或豬絞肉均可使用。

Either ground beef or ground pork
may be used in this recipe.

茄子碎肉飯 2人份

	圓茄子或長茄子···	450公克 (12兩)
	絞肉·····················	150公克 (4兩)
①	葱、薑末··············	各2大匙
	蒜末····················	1大匙
	辣椒醬··················	1小匙
②	醬油····················	4大匙
	料酒、糖··············	各2小匙
	水或高湯··············	4大匙
	太白粉··················	½大匙
	葱花····················	4大匙
	飯·······················	2碗

❶茄子去皮，切長條，放入多量水內浸泡備用（使用時瀝乾水份）。

❷油３大匙燒熱，炒香①料隨入絞肉炒熟後，放入茄子翻炒數分鐘至軟，再加②料燒開攪拌成濃稠狀，上灑葱花即可加在飯上與蔬菜配食。

EGGPLANT WITH GROUND PORK OVER RICE SERVES 2

1 lb. (450 g.) round
  or long eggplant
1/3 lb. (150 g.) ground pork

① 2 T. each: green onion,
    ginger root; both minced
  1 T. garlic, minced
  1 t. chili paste

② 4 T. soy sauce
  2 t. each: cooking wine
    or sherry, sugar
  4 T. stock or water
  1/2 T. cornstarch

4 T. green onion, chopped
2 c. cooked rice

❶ Peel the eggplant and cut into long, thick strips (2-1/2" × 3/4" or 6×2 cm). Soak in water and set aside. (Drain thoroughly before use.)

❷ Heat 3 tablespoons oil in a preheated wok. Stir-fry ① until fragrant. Add the ground pork and stir-fry until cooked through. Add the eggplant and stir-fry several minutes until soft. Add ② and bring to a boil. When a thick sauce has formed, sprinkle the chopped green onion over the top. Serve over rice with vegetables.

蝦米先洗淨，再泡水約10分鐘後使用。
Wash the dried shrimp and soak in water for about 10 minutes before use.

生紅葱頭。
Raw shallots.

市面上有炸好紅葱頭，加入菜或湯內增加香味。
Fried shallots are available commercially. They add rich flavor to stir-fried dishes and soups.

什錦炊飯 6人份

①	米	3杯
	紅葱頭（切薄片）	3粒
	蝦米（泡水）	2大匙
	瘦肉（切丁）	4兩
	香菇（泡水，切丁）	3朵
	醬油	3大匙
②	水	4杯
	塩	⅔小匙
	胡椒	少許
③	紅蘿蔔（切丁）青豆仁	共2杯

❶米洗淨泡水1小時後瀝乾備用。
❷油4大匙燒熱，將紅葱頭炒香，依序放入①料炒香並加醬油3大匙以增加香味，再加②料燒滾後放入米及③料，以小火一邊翻拌一邊蓋鍋燜煮，反覆煮到米熟即可。煮出的飯旣有彈性又香，但需時時注意否則易燒焦。
■也可直接用電鍋來煮飯，但②料內的水需減爲3杯。電鍋煮飯很方便不易燒焦，但煮出的飯較無彈性。
■也可用糯米來煮，但水份需減少¼的量。

LITTLE-OF-EVERYTHING RICE SERVES 6

3 c. raw rice
3 shallots, thinly sliced
① 2 T. small dried shrimp, soaked
1/3 lb. (150 g.) lean pork,
  cut into 3/4" (1.75 cm) cubes
3 dried Chinese black
  mushrooms,
  soaked and cubed
3 T. soy sauce
② 4 c. water
2/3 t. salt
pinch of pepper
③ total of 2 c.: carrot, cubed; peas

❶ Wash the rice. Soak for one hour, drain, and set aside.
❷ Heat 4 tablespoons of oil in a preheated wok. Stir-fry the shallots until fragrant. Add the ingredients in ① one by one and stir-fry until fragrant. Add the soy sauce for extra flavor, then add ② and bring to a boil. Add the rice and ③. Cover and simmer, stirring frequently, until the rice is done. The rice will be delicious and springy in texture. It is important to watch the rice constantly while it is cooking to prevent scorching.
■ The rice may also be cooked in an electric rice cooker, but reduce the water in ② to 3 cups. An electric rice cooker is convenient and less likely to scorch the rice, but the texture of the rice will be less springy.
■ Glutinous rice (also called sweet rice or mochi rice) may also be used in this recipe. Reduce the water used by one quarter.

蝦米先洗淨再泡水約10分鐘後使用。
Wash the dried shrimp and soak 10 minutes before use.

餛飩皮切絲用油炸灑在粥上，增加香味。如一次炸多些可保存在罐內，一、二星期不壞，也可用來拌沙拉。
Cut the wonton skins into strips and deep-fry. They provide an interesting flavor and texture contrast when sprinkled over the congee. They may be kept in a covered container for a week or two.

如用炸油條，也先切粒再炸。
If you use fried Chinese crullers, cut in pieces before use.

牛肉粥 ^{4人份}

米‧‧‧‧‧‧‧‧‧‧‧‧‧‧‧‧‧‧‧‧‧‧‧‧‧‧‧ 1杯
牛肉(切片)‧‧‧‧‧‧‧‧‧‧‧225公克(6兩)

① 水‧‧‧‧‧‧‧‧‧‧‧‧‧‧‧‧‧‧‧‧‧‧‧‧‧‧ 2大匙
醬油、太白粉‧‧‧‧‧‧‧‧‧‧‧ 各1大匙
料酒‧‧‧‧‧‧‧‧‧‧‧‧‧‧‧‧‧‧‧‧‧‧‧‧ ½大匙

② 乾蝦米‧‧‧‧‧‧‧‧‧‧‧‧‧‧‧‧‧‧‧‧ 2大匙
蒜瓣(拍破)‧‧‧‧‧‧‧‧‧‧‧‧‧‧‧ 2粒
醬油‧‧‧‧‧‧‧‧‧‧‧‧‧‧‧‧‧‧‧‧‧‧‧‧ ½大匙
高湯(或水)‧‧‧‧‧‧‧‧‧‧‧‧‧‧10杯

③ 塩‧‧‧‧‧‧‧‧‧‧‧‧‧‧‧‧‧‧‧‧‧‧‧‧‧‧ 1⅓小匙
胡椒‧‧‧‧‧‧‧‧‧‧‧‧‧‧‧‧‧‧‧‧‧‧‧‧ 少許

④ 葱絲‧‧‧‧‧‧‧‧‧‧‧‧‧‧‧‧‧‧‧‧‧‧‧ 2大匙
薑絲‧‧‧‧‧‧‧‧‧‧‧‧‧‧‧‧‧‧‧‧‧‧‧ 1大匙

炸餛飩皮絲(或炸油條)‧‧‧‧‧‧‧ 1杯
香菜或芹菜(切碎)‧‧‧‧‧‧‧‧‧‧ 4大匙

❶米洗淨,牛肉調①料拌醃。蝦米泡水10分鐘瀝乾水份。

❷油2大匙燒熱,將②料炒香加醬油½大匙增加香味,放入高湯及米燒開後,改小火煮40分鐘至湯汁呈糊狀,將牛肉一片一片放入,加③料調味並試鹹淡,食時撒上④料、炸餛飩皮絲及香菜即可。

■也可將牛肉片改用牛絞肉做成丸子來煮。

■炸餛飩皮絲僅爲增加香味,如無可免用。

■粥燒煮時偶而需攪動以免黏鍋。

BEEF CONGEE SERVES 4

1 c. raw rice
1/2 lb. (225 g.) beef, sliced

① 2 T. water
1 T. each: soy sauce, cornstarch
1/2 T. cooking wine or sherry

② 2 T. small dried shrimp
2 cloves garlic, smashed
1/2 T. soy sauce
10 c. stock (or water)

③ 1-1/3 t. salt
pinch of pepper

④ 2 T. green onion, finely shredded
1 T. ginger root, finely shredded

1 c. fried wonton skin strips
or fried Chinese crullers (油條)
4 T. fresh coriander leaves,
or celery, minced

❶ Wash the rice. Marinate the beef in ①. Soak the dried shrimp in water for 10 minutes and drain.

❷ Heat 2 tablespoons oil in a preheated wok. Stir-fry ② until fragrant. Add 1/2 tablespoon soy sauce for extra flavor. Add the stock or water and the rice and bring to a boil. Cook over low heat for 40 minutes until thickened. Put the beef in slice by slice. Add ③ to taste. Sprinkle on ④ and the fried wonton skin strips and coriander leaves before serving.

■ Ground beef made into meatballs and cooked in the congee may be substituted for the beef slices.

■ The fried wonton skin strips are for extra flavor and texture contrast. They may be omitted if unavailable.

■ Stir the congee occasionally while cooking to prevent sticking.

蛤蜊有時含沙，故宜先煮過去殼後
使用為佳。
Clams often contain sand, so it is
preferable to cook them first and
remove the meat from the shells.

蝦也可去殼後使用。
The shrimp may also be shelled
before use.

生蠔有新鮮的更好，如無可用冰凍
的。
Fresh oysters are best, but frozen
are also good.

三鮮粥 4 人份

① 米⋯⋯⋯⋯⋯⋯⋯⋯⋯⋯⋯ 1杯
　 水⋯⋯⋯⋯⋯⋯⋯⋯⋯⋯⋯ 7杯

② 蛤蜊(取肉)⋯⋯⋯⋯⋯⋯⋯12個
　 蝦(洗淨，去沙腸)⋯⋯⋯⋯12隻
　 生蠔(洗淨)⋯⋯⋯⋯⋯⋯⋯12個
　 薑(切碎)⋯⋯⋯⋯⋯⋯⋯⋯½大匙

③ 煮蛤蜊湯⋯⋯⋯⋯⋯⋯⋯⋯ 1½杯
　 塩⋯⋯⋯⋯⋯⋯⋯⋯⋯⋯⋯ 1小匙
　 料酒⋯⋯⋯⋯⋯⋯⋯⋯⋯⋯ 1大匙
　 胡椒⋯⋯⋯⋯⋯⋯⋯⋯⋯⋯少許

　 芹菜或葱(切碎)⋯⋯⋯⋯⋯ 2大匙
　 嫩薑絲⋯⋯⋯⋯⋯⋯⋯⋯⋯ 2大匙

❶米洗淨，加水７杯浸泡30分鐘。蛤蜊洗淨，加水１½杯煮到蛤蜊開口立即熄火，取出蛤蜊肉用在②料內，湯汁濾去渣後用在③料內。

❷將①料燒煮15分鐘至米熟即可，放入②料及③料再煮開，試鹹淡，食時加芹菜末即成。

■三鮮粥②的材料沒有限制，如鮮魷魚、蟹、墨魚、魚肉等都可取代。

■嫩薑絲如無可免用。

SEAFOOD CONGEE SERVES 4

① 1 c. raw rice
　 7 c. water

② 12 clams, shucked
　 12 shrimp, washed and
　　　deveined
　 12 oysters, washed
　 1/2 T. ginger root, finely minced

③ 1-1/2 c. clam broth
　 1 t. salt
　 1 T. cooking wine or sherry
　 pinch of pepper

　 2 T. celery or green onion,
　　　minced
　 2 T. young ginger root,
　　　finely shredded

❶ Wash the rice. Add the 7 cups of water and soak for 30 minutes. Wash the clams, put in a pot with 1-1/2 cups water, and cook until the shells open. Turn off the heat. Remove the meat from the shells for ②, and strain the broth for use in ③.

❷ Cook ① for 15 minutes, until the rice is done. Add ② and ③ and bring to a boil. Season to taste. Sprinkle the minced celery over the top before serving.

■ Any kind of seafood may be used in ②, for example, fresh cuttlefish, crabmeat, squid, fish fillets, and so forth.

■ The shredded young ginger root may be omitted if unavailable.

五香粉是一種香料，也可用胡椒取代。

Pepper may be substituted for the five-spice powder.

酸菜切絲如覺太鹹，泡水５分鐘再使用。

Shred the salt rape greens. Soak 5 minutes before use if they are too salty.

③料內的高湯如是用罐頭高湯，塩要略減。

If you use canned chicken stock in ③, reduce the amount of salt used.

鶏腿湯麵 4人份

①	鶏腿⋯⋯⋯⋯⋯	4隻900公克(1斤半)
	太白粉、醬油⋯⋯⋯⋯⋯⋯	各1½大匙
	糖、料酒⋯⋯⋯⋯⋯⋯⋯	各½大匙
	塩⋯⋯⋯⋯⋯⋯⋯⋯⋯	½小匙
	五香粉(或胡椒)⋯⋯⋯⋯	⅓小匙
	蛋⋯⋯⋯⋯⋯⋯⋯⋯⋯	1個
	太白粉⋯⋯⋯⋯⋯⋯⋯	4大匙
	「炸油」⋯⋯⋯⋯⋯⋯⋯	適量
	酸菜或雪菜(切碎)⋯⋯⋯	1½杯
②	辣椒絲⋯⋯⋯⋯⋯⋯⋯	½大匙
	塩、糖⋯⋯⋯⋯⋯⋯⋯	各½小匙
	麻油⋯⋯⋯⋯⋯⋯⋯⋯	½小匙
③	葱末⋯⋯⋯⋯⋯⋯⋯	2大匙
	醬油⋯⋯⋯⋯⋯⋯⋯	2大匙
	塩、麻油⋯⋯⋯⋯⋯	各1小匙
	胡椒⋯⋯⋯⋯⋯⋯⋯	少許
	高湯或滾水⋯⋯⋯⋯	8杯
	乾麵條⋯⋯⋯⋯⋯	300公克(8兩)

(③料 四人份)

❶鶏腿用刀在中間直劃開(易入味,也容易炸熟),加①料拌匀。炸前拌入蛋,再沾上多量太白粉。
❷油２大匙燒熱,放入酸菜略炒,再入②料炒匀盛出。
❸「炸油」燒熱,將鶏腿炸至表面呈金黃色(約８分鐘)撈出。③料調好備用。
❹多量水燒開,放入麵條煮約４分鐘撈出(麵的煮法參考第6頁)
❺各麵碗內放入③料及煮熟麵條,並加上酸菜及炸鶏腿即成。

排骨湯麵:將炸鶏腿改用炸排骨,其他做法與鶏腿麵同。炸排骨做法:大排骨４片(600公克1斤),兩面拍鬆,加水２大匙以⅔①料拌醃,拌入蛋再沾太白粉油炸４分鐘即成。

CHICKEN LEGS WITH NOODLES IN BROTH SERVES 4

①
- 4 chicken legs (2 lb. or 900 g.)
- 1-1/2 T. each: cornstarch, soy sauce
- 1/2 T. each: sugar, cooking wine or sherry
- 1/2 t. salt
- 1/3 t. five-spice powder (or pepper)
- 1 egg
- 4 T. cornstarch
- oil for deep-frying
- 1-1/2 c. pickled mustard cabbage or salt rape greens

②
- 1/2 T. hot red pepper, shredded
- 1/2 t. each: salt, sugar
- 1/2 t. sesame oil

③
- 4 Servings:
- 2 T. green onion, minced
- 2 T. soy sauce
- 1 t. each: salt, sesame oil
- pinch of pepper
- 8 c. stock or boiling water
- 2/3 lb. (300 g.) dry noodles

❶ Slash the chicken leg in the center. (This helps it better absorb the seasoning, and to deep-fry faster.) Marinate in ①. Dip in egg, then in cornstarch before deep-frying.
❷ Heat 2 tablespoons oil in a preheated wok. Stir-fry the pickled mustard cabbage or salt rape greens briefly. Add ②, stir-fry briefly, and remove from wok.
❸ Heat the oil for deep-frying. Fry the chicken legs until the skin is golden brown, about 8 minutes. Remove. Mix ③ and set aside.
❹ Cook the noodles in boiling water for about 4 minutes, until done. (See p. 6 for directions on how to cook noodles.)
❺ Divide ③ among four serving bowls, and add one-fourth of the cooked noodles to each. Put some of the vegetable and one chicken leg in each bowl of noodles. Serve.

Pork Chops with Noodles in Broth
Use pork chops instead of the chicken legs, and proceed as above. Pound both sides of four pork chops (1 lb. 5 oz. or 600 g.) until tender. Add 2 tablespoons water and 2/3 of ① to marinate. Mix in the egg, then dredge in cornstarch. Deep-fry about 4 minutes.

略有肥肉參雜在內的肉，燒出來比較嫩，如牛腩、筋條等。
Fat-marbled beef, such as beef sinews or tendons, will be more tender.

豆瓣醬：黃豆和麵粉經過煮熟酸酵製成。
Bean paste is made by the fermentation of cooked soy beans and flour.

辣豆瓣醬：用辣椒加豆瓣釀製而成。亦可用辣椒醬取代。
Hot bean paste is bean paste made with hot peppers. Chili paste may be substituted.

豆瓣牛肉麵 6人份

	牛肉	900公克 (1斤8兩)
①	葱(切段)	3枝
	薑	3片
	蒜瓣	3粒
	醬油	¾杯
②	黑豆瓣醬	1½大匙
	辣豆瓣醬	1½小匙
	水	8杯
③	料酒	2大匙
	糖	1大匙
	八角	2粒
	葱(切粒)	½大匙
	醬油	1小匙
④	麻油	¼小匙
	胡椒	少許
	紅燒牛肉汁、滾水	各1杯
	青菜	450公克 (12兩)
	乾麵條	450公克 (12兩)

※④料為一人份

❶牛肉洗淨，切成4公分之塊狀。

❷油2大匙燒熱，將①、②料按順序放入炒香，再入③料及牛肉燒開，改小火續煮約1小時至牛肉爛湯汁剩約6杯，即成紅燒牛肉。

❸多量水燒開，先將青菜放入燙熟撈出。再放入麵條煮約4分鐘至熟撈出(麵的煮法參考第6頁)。

❹麵碗內放入④料、煮熟麵條及青菜，再加上適量的紅燒牛肉即成。

BEAN PASTE-FLAVORED BEEF WITH NOODLES IN BROTH SERVES 6

①	2 lb. (900 g.) beef
	3 green onions, cut in 1-1/4" (3 cm) sections
	3 slices ginger root
	3 cloves garlic
②	3/4 c. soy sauce
	1-1/2 T. bean paste
	1-1/2 t. hot bean paste
③	8 c. water
	2 T. cooking wine or sherry
	1 T. sugar
	2 flowerets star anise
④	1 Serving:
	1/2 T. green onion, diced
	1 t. soy sauce
	1/4 t. sesame oil
	pinch of pepper
	1 c. each: liquid from cooking the beef in step ❷, boiling water
	1 lb. (450 g.) vegetable of your choice
	1 lb. (450 g.) dry noodles

❶ Wash the beef and cut into 1-1/2" (4 cm) cubes.

❷ Heat 2 tablespoons oil in a preheated wok. Add the ingredients of ① and ② one by one in order and stir-fry until fragrant. Add ③ and the beef and bring to a boil. Simmer over low heat about one hour until the meat is cooked soft and the liquid is reduced to 6 cups. Retain the liquid for use in ④.

❸ Fill a pot a little over half-full with water and bring to a boil. Blanch the vegetable in the boiling water until just cooked. Remove. Cook the noodles in this water until done, about 4 minutes. (See p. 6 for directions on how to cook noodles.) Remove.

❹ Put ④ in each of 6 serving bowls. Put one portion of the noodles, vegetable, and beef in each bowl and serve.

買來剁好的牛尾做起來方便。
Buy pre-cut oxtail to save time and trouble.

八角：又名大茴香，也是常用香料之一種。
Star anise is another frequently used spice in Chinese cooking.

花椒：中國料理常用香料之一種。
Szechuan peppercorns are a frequently used seasoning in Chinese cooking.

清燉牛尾湯麵 3人份

①		
	牛尾··················	900公克(1斤半)
	薑··················	5大片
	葱··················	2枝
	花椒··················	10粒
	八角··················	1朵
	料酒··················	3大匙
	水··················	8杯
	塩··················	1小匙

②		
	葱(切粒)··················	½大匙
	醬油··················	1小匙
	麻油··················	¼小匙
	胡椒··················	適量

一人份

青菜··················	450公克(12兩)
乾麵條··················	225公克(6兩)

❶牛尾切塊，在滾水內川燙後，放入①料內燒開，改小火燒煮約2小時，至肉熟軟，餘汁剩約6杯，加塩試鹹淡備用。

❷水6杯燒開，先將青菜燙熟撈出，再放入麵條煮約4分鐘至熟撈出(麵的煮法參考第6頁)。

❸各麵碗內放入②料、牛尾湯、及煮熟麵條、青菜再加上適量的牛尾即成。

STEWED OXTAIL WITH NOODLES IN BROTH SERVES 3

① 2 lb. (900 g.) oxtail
5 large slices ginger root
2 green onions
10 Szechuan peppercorns
1 floweret star anise
3 T. cooking wine or sherry
8 c. water
1 t. salt

② 1 Serving:
1/2 T. green onion, chopped
1 t. soy sauce
1/4 t. sesame oil
pepper, as desired

1 lb. (450 g.) vegetable
of your choice
1/2 lb. (225 g.) dry noodles

❶ Cut the oxtail into chunks and blanch in boiling water. Remove. Put the beef in a pot with ①. Bring to a boil, then simmer over low heat for 2 hours until the meat is cooked soft and the liquid is reduced to 6 cups. Add salt to taste. Set aside.

❷ Bring 6 cups water to a boil. Blanch the vegetable in it until just cooked; remove. Cook the noodles in this water until done, about 4 minutes. (See p. 6 for directions on how to cook noodles.) Remove.

❸ Put ② in each serving bowl, then one portion of the oxtail broth, vegetable, and cooked noodles. Top with cooked oxtail chunks and serve.

筍有切好片的罐頭用來方便。
Use presliced canned bamboo
shoots for extra convenience.

乾金針菜½杯，泡好後漲大為 1 杯。
One half cup of dried lily flowers
will expand to fill one cup after
soaking.

乾木耳¼杯，泡好後漲大約 1 杯。
One quarter cup of dried wood
ears will also expand to fill about
one cup after soaking.

大魯麵 2人份

	豬瘦肉 (切片) ········	150公克 (4兩)
①	醬油、水············	各2小匙
	太白粉··············	2小匙
	番茄 (切塊) ··········	1個
	高湯或水············	5杯
②	醬油··············	1大匙
	鹽················	1小匙
	麻油、胡椒··········	各少許
	青江菜 (略切) ·······	4棵
	筍 (切薄片) ·········	½杯
③	乾金針菜············	½杯
	乾木耳··············	¼杯
	香菇··············	2大朵
④	太白粉··············	3大匙
	水················	5大匙
	蛋 (打散) ···········	2個
	乾麵條·············	150公克 (4兩)

❶肉片加①料調勻備用。③料內之金針菜泡水去硬蒂頭，木耳泡軟，香菇泡水切片。

❷油2大匙燒熱，將肉炒熟盛出。再加油2大匙炒番茄，並加②料及③料燒開，放回炒熟肉片，再以④料勾芡成薄糊狀，最後把蛋汁徐徐倒入，立即熄火。

❸多量水燒開放入麵條煮約4分鐘至熟，分盛在麵碗內 (麵的煮法參考第6頁)，將做好的湯料澆在麵上即可食。

■如愛食辣者可酌加辣豆瓣醬少許，另加些蒜末味更佳。

LITTLE-OF-EVERYTHING NOODLE SOUP SERVES 2

① 1/3 lb. (150 g.) lean pork, sliced
2 t. each: soy sauce, water
2 t. cornstarch
1 tomato, cubed

② 5 c. stock or water
1 T. soy sauce
1 t. salt
few drops sesame oil
pinch of pepper

③ 5 stalks bok choy,
  cut in bite-size pieces
1/2 c. bamboo shoots,
  thinly sliced
1/2 c. dried lily flowers (金針)
1/4 c. dried wood ears (木耳)
2 large dried Chinese black
  mushrooms

④ 3 T. cornstarch
5 T. water
2 eggs, lightly beaten
1/3 lb. (150 g.) dry noodles

❶ Marinate the pork slices in ① and set aside. Soak the dried lilies and remove the hard ends. Soak the wood ears until soft. Soak the dried black mushrooms until soft and cut into thick strips.

❷ Heat 2 tablespoons oil in a preheated wok. Stir-fry the pork slices until done and remove. Heat another 2 tablespoons oil and stir-fry the tomato. Add ② and ③ and bring to a boil. Return the pork to the wok. Add ④ to slightly thicken the broth. Finally, pour the beaten egg into the broth in a slow stream. Turn off the heat.

❸ Fill a pot a little over half-full with water and bring to a boil. Add the noodles and cook until done, about 4 minutes. (See p. 6 for directions on how to cook noodles.) Put half of the noodles in each of two serving bowls. Pour some of the soup over the top of each and serve.

■ If you like your noodles spicier, add a little hot bean paste and some minced garlic to the noodles before eating.

榨菜使用時先洗去外面辛香料。
Wash the pickled mustard greens before use to reduce the saltiness.

切片再切絲，因很鹹須放入水內泡
10分鐘後略擠出水份再使用。
Slice first, then shred. Because of its saltiness, it must be soaked for 10 minutes. Squeeze out the excess moisture before use.

乾麵條可存放很久用來方便。
Dry noodles have a conveniently long shelf life.

榨菜肉絲湯麵 2人份

①	豬瘦肉(切絲)‧‧‧‧‧‧‧‧‧‧150公克(4兩)	
	醬油、料酒‧‧‧‧‧‧‧‧‧‧‧‧‧太白粉‧‧‧‧‧‧‧‧‧‧‧‧‧‧‧	各2小匙
	葱末‧‧‧‧‧‧‧‧‧‧‧‧‧‧‧‧‧‧‧½大匙	
	榨菜(切絲)‧‧‧‧‧‧‧‧‧‧‧‧‧¾杯	
②	水‧‧‧‧‧‧‧‧‧‧‧‧‧‧‧‧‧‧‧1大匙	
	醬油‧‧‧‧‧‧‧‧‧‧‧‧‧‧‧‧‧1小匙	
	糖‧‧‧‧‧‧‧‧‧‧‧‧‧‧‧‧‧‧½小匙	
	胡椒‧‧‧‧‧‧‧‧‧‧‧‧‧‧‧‧‧少許	
③	葱末‧‧‧‧‧‧‧‧‧‧‧‧‧‧‧1大匙	二人份
	醬油‧‧‧‧‧‧‧‧‧‧‧‧‧‧‧1大匙	
	塩、麻油‧‧‧‧‧‧‧‧各½小匙	
	胡椒‧‧‧‧‧‧‧‧‧‧‧‧‧‧‧少許	
	高湯或滾水‧‧‧‧‧‧‧‧‧‧‧4杯	
	青菜‧‧‧‧‧‧‧‧‧‧‧‧‧‧‧‧‧‧4棵	
	乾麵條‧‧‧‧‧‧‧‧‧‧‧‧150公克(4兩)	

❶肉絲加①料調勻，炒前拌入½大匙油則肉易炒散開。

❷油2大匙燒熱，將葱炒香，放入肉絲炒熟，加入榨菜及②料拌炒均勻盛出。③料調好備用。

❸多量水燒開，先將青菜放入燙熟撈出。再放入麵條煮約4分鐘至熟撈出(麵的煮法參考第6頁)。

❹麵碗內各放入③料、燙熟青菜及煮熟麵條，最後放上榨菜肉絲即成。

PICKLED MUSTARD AND PORK SHRED NOODLE SOUP SERVES 2

①	1/3 lb. (150 g.) lean pork, shredded
	2 t. each: soy sauce, cooking wine or sherry, cornstarch
	1/2 T. green onion, minced
	3/4 c. Szechuan pickled mustard greens, shredded
②	1 T. water
	1 t. soy sauce
	1/2 t. sugar
	pinch of pepper
③	2 Servings:
	1 T. green onion, minced
	1 T. soy sauce
	1/2 t. each: salt, sesame oil
	pinch of pepper
	4 c. stock or boiling water
	4 stalks green vegetable, cut in bite-size pieces
	1/3 lb. (150 g.) dry noodles

❶ Marinate the pork shreds in ①. Mix in 1/2 tablespoon oil before stir-frying so that the shreds will separate easily.

❷ Heat 2 tablespoons oil in a preheated wok. Stir-fry the green onion until fragrant. Add the pork shreds and stir-fry until done. Add the pickled mustard greens and ②. Stir-fry until the ingredients are evenly coated with sauce. Mix ③ and set aside.

❸ Fill a pot a little more than half full with water and bring to a boil. Blanch the vegetable until just cooked. Remove. Cook the noodles in the water until done, about 4 minutes. (See p. 6 for directions on how to cook noodles.) Remove.

❹ Put half of ③ in each of two serving bowls, then the vegetable, the noodles, and finally the pickled mustard and pork shreds. Serve.

将油菜、芥菜或白蘿蔔莖12兩，洗淨晾乾。
Wash 1 lb. (450 g.) of rape greens, mustard greens, or white radish greens, and spread out to dry.

灑上塩 1 大匙，搓揉至軟，醃一天以上，使用前略洗，擠乾水份剁碎即可使用。
Sprinkle 1 tablespoon salt over the greens and rub in until the vegetable is soft. Cure for one day or longer and it is ready for use. Wash, squeeze out excess moisture, and chop before use.

市面上有做好的雪菜，用來方便。
Commercially prepared salt rape greens are available and convenient to use.

雪菜肉絲湯麵 2人份

① 豬瘦肉（切絲）········150公克（4兩）

① { 醬油、料酒············· 各2小匙
太白粉·············

葱、辣椒（切碎）·············½大匙
雪菜（切碎）············· 1½杯

② 水············· 1大匙
糖、麻油·············各½小匙
塩·············⅓小匙
胡椒·············少許

③ 葱末············· 1大匙
醬油············· 1大匙
塩、麻油·············各½小匙
胡椒·············少許
高湯或滾水············· 4杯
乾麵條·············150公克（4兩）

二人份

❶ 肉絲加①料調勻，炒前拌入½大匙油則肉易炒散開。

❷ 油2大匙燒熱，將肉絲炒熟盛出。再加1大匙油放入葱、辣椒及雪菜略炒，並加入肉絲及②料炒勻即可盛出。③料調好備用。

❸ 多量水燒開，放入麵條煮約4分鐘至熟撈出（麵的煮法參考第6頁）。

❹ 麵碗內各放入③料、高湯及煮熟的麵條，再放上雪菜肉絲即成。

■ 雪菜略鹹，使用前略洗，擠乾水份剁碎即可用。

SALT RAPE GREENS AND PORK SHRED NOODLE SOUP SERVES 2

① 1/3 lb. (150 g.) lean pork, shredded
2 t. each: soy sauce, cooking wine or sherry, cornstarch

1/2 T. each: green onion, hot red pepper; both shredded
1-1/2 c. salt rape greens, chopped

② 1 T. water
1/2 t. each: sugar, sesame oil
1/3 t. salt
pinch of pepper

③ 2 Servings:
1 T. green onion, minced
1 T. soy sauce
1/2 t. each: salt, sesame oil
pinch of pepper
4 c. stock or boiling water
1/3 lb. (150 g.) dry noodles

❶ Marinate the pork shreds in ①. Mix in 1/2 tablespoon oil before stir-frying so that the meat shreds will separate easily.

❷ Heat 2 tablespoons oil in a preheated wok. Stir-fry the meat shreds until cooked through and remove. Add another tablespoon oil to the wok and stir-fry the green onion, hot red pepper, and salt rape greens briefly. Add the pork shreds and ② and stir-fry until well combined. Remove. Mix ③ and set aside.

❸ Fill a pot a little over half-full with water. Bring to a boil and cook the noodles in it until done, about 4 minutes. (See p. 6 for directions on how to cook noodles.) Remove.

❹ Put half of ③ in each of two serving bowls, along with the soup stock, cooked noodles, and the salt rape greens with pork shreds. Serve.

■ Salt rape greens are very salty and must be washed before use. Squeeze out the excess moisture and chop.

此菜餚若用蛋麵來做更理想。若無，用普通麵做也可。

Egg noodles are especially good in this dish, but if unavailable, use regular noodles.

香菇及洋葱是炒香用的。

The dried black mushrooms and onion are stir-fried until fragrant and tasty.

加入豆芽菜及韭黃，香香脆脆的特別有風味。但不宜煮過久，做好後應馬上食用。

The mung bean sprouts and yellow Chinese chives add a delicious flavor and crunchy texture. Be careful not to cook them too long. Serve immediately after cooking.

韭黃燴麵 2人份

瘦肉 (豬、牛或雞肉、切絲) ……
…………………150公克 (4兩)
① 醬油、料酒……………… 各2小匙
太白粉……………………… 2小匙
② 香菇 (泡軟、切絲)……………… 2朶
洋葱 (切絲)…………………… 1杯
水……………………………… 2杯
筍 (切絲)…………………… ½杯
③ 醬油…………………………… 1大匙
塩、糖……………………… 各¾小匙
胡椒……………………………… 少許
太白粉……………………… 1½大匙
豆芽菜………………………… 1杯
韭黃 (切2.5公分長)………… 1杯
乾麵……………………150公克 (4兩)

❶肉絲加①料調勻,炒前拌入1大匙油則肉易炒散開。
❷油2大匙燒熱,先將肉絲炒熟撈出,再加油2大匙燒熱,放入②料炒香,續入③料燒開,攪拌成濃汁,放回肉絲再燒開後加入豆芽菜及韭黃拌勻即離火。
❸麵煮熟盛在盤內,把煮好的料趁熱淋在麵上即成。

煮麵法:半鍋水燒開,放入麵條,再燒開後改小火,煮約4分鐘至熟即撈出 (麵的煮法參考第6頁),如加1大匙油略拌,可免麵條黏在一起。如麵需加熱,可放入烤箱燒炙約12分鐘至略焦黃。或用少許油將麵兩面煎黃味更佳。

YELLOW CHINESE CHIVES IN SOY SAUCE OVER NOODLES SERVES 2

1/3 lb. (150 g.) lean pork, beef, or chicken, shredded
① 2 t. each: soy sauce, cooking wine or sherry
2 t. cornstarch
② 2 dried Chinese black mushrooms, soaked and cut in julienne strips
1 c. onion, sliced in thin half-circles
③ 2 c. water
1/2 c. bamboo shoots, shredded
1 T. soy sauce
3/4 t. each: salt, sugar
pinch of pepper
1-1/2 T. cornstarch
1 c. mung bean sprouts
1 c. yellow Chinese chives (韭黃), cut in 1" (2.5 cm) sections
1/3 lb. (150 g.) dry noodles

❶ Marinate the meat shreds in ①. Mix in one tablespoon oil before stir-frying so that they will separate easily.
❷ Heat 2 tablespoons oil in a preheated wok. Stir-fry the meat shreds until done and remove. Heat another 2 tablespoons oil. Stir-fry ② until fragrant. Add ③, bring to a boil, and stir to form a thick sauce. Return the meat shreds to the wok and heat until bubbly. Put in the bean sprouts and yellow Chinese chives. Stir to coat evenly with the sauce. Remove from heat.
❸ Put a portion of cooked noodles in each serving bowl and top with the stir-fried mixture. Serve.

How to Cook Noodles:
Fill a pot a little more than half-full with water and bring to a boil. Put in the noodles. After the water begins to boil again, lower the heat. Cook until done, about 4 minutes, and remove noodles from water. (See p. 6 for directions on how to cook noodles.) Mix 1 tablespoon oil into the cooked noodles to prevent their sticking together. To reheat the noodles, place in a baking pan and turn the oven to "broil." Bake about 12 minutes, until the noodles turn golden brown. Frying the noodles in a small amount of oil until golden will also give the noodles a different and delicious taste.

白菜切長條。
Cut the Chinese cabbage in long strips.

芹菜切長條。
Cut the celery in long strips.

洋菇切片。
Cut the fresh mushrooms in slices.

蝦仁燴麵 ^{2人份}

	蝦仁	112.5公克（3兩）
①	太白粉	1小匙
	料酒	½小匙
	塩	⅛小匙
	瘦肉（切片）	112.5公克（3兩）
②	醬油、水	各½大匙
	太白粉	
	葱、薑末	各1大匙
③	白菜（切長條）	2杯
	芹菜（切長條）	1杯
	洋菇（切片）	½杯
	水	2杯
	醬油	1大匙
④	塩、糖	各¾小匙
	胡椒	少許
	太白粉	1½大匙
	乾麵	150公克（4兩）

❶蝦仁處理乾淨瀝乾水份，加①料調拌，肉片加②料拌勻。

❷油2大匙燒熱，將蝦炒熟撈出，再加油2大匙燒熱，將肉片亦炒熟撈出。另加1大匙油燒熱，炒青葱、薑末，再依序放入③料略炒，加④料燒開成濃稠狀，放回肉片及蝦仁，拌勻即成。

❸麵煮熟盛在盤內，把煮好的料趁熱淋在麵上即成。

■煮麵法參考第71頁韭黃燴麵。

SHRIMP IN SAUCE OVER NOODLES SERVES 2

	1/4 lb. (112.5 g.) shrimp, shelled	
①	1 t. cornstarch	
	1/2 t. cooking wine or sherry	
	1/8 t. salt	
	1/4 lb. (112.5 g.) lean pork, sliced	
②	1/2 T. each: soy sauce, water, cornstarch	
	1 T. each: green onion, ginger root; both minced	
③	2 c. Chinese cabbage (Nappa), cut in long strips	
	1 c. celery, cut in long strips	
	1/2 c. fresh mushrooms, sliced	
	2 c. water	
	1 T. soy sauce	
④	3/4 t. each: salt, sugar	
	pinch of pepper	
	1-1/2 T. cornstarch	
	1/3 lb. (150 g.) dry noodles	

❶ Wash the shrimp, drain, and pat dry with paper towels. Marinate in ①. Marinate the pork slices in ②.

❷ Heat 2 tablespoons oil in a preheated wok. Stir-fry the shrimp until done and remove. Heat another 2 tablespoons oil. Stir-fry the pork slices until done and remove. Heat another tablespoon oil and stir-fry the minced green onion and ginger root until fragrant. Add the ingredients in ③ one by one in order and stir-fry briefly. Add ④ and heat until bubbly and a thick sauce forms. Return the pork slices and shrimp to the wok. Stir-fry briefly and remove.

❸ Cook the noodles and put on serving plates. Top with the stir-fried mixture and serve.

■ See p. 71, Yellow Chinese Chives in Soy Sauce over Noodles, for how to cook the noodles.

粗白麵是用漂白過的麵粉製成，如是真空包裝，則用滾水略川燙，攪散撈出使用，亦可用其他任何麵來代替。

Broad noodles are made with bleached flour. If using vacuum-pack noodles, then immerse the noodles briefly in boiling water, and remove. Any other type of noodles may also be used in this dish.

蝦仁處理乾淨，加①料拌醃。

Clean the shrimp and marinate in ①.

洋蔥切絲，番茄切塊。

Slice the onion thinly, then cut the rounds in half and separate the rings. Cut the tomato into chunks.

蝦仁炒粗麵 ^{2人份}

	熟粗白麵 ·············	450公克 (12兩)
	蝦仁 ·················	225公克 (6兩)
①	料酒 ·················	½大匙
	太白粉 ···············	2小匙
	塩 ··················	¼小匙
	洋葱 (切絲) ···········	1½杯
	番茄 (切塊) ···········	1杯
	醬油 ·················	2大匙
	葱 (切段) ·············	2枝
	水 ··················	½杯
②	糖 ··················	1½小匙
	太白粉 ···············	1小匙
	塩 ··················	⅓小匙
	味精、胡椒 ···········	適量

❶蝦仁處理乾淨，加①料拌醃。
❷油3大匙燒熱，入蝦仁炒熟盛出。再加油1大匙燒熱，炒香洋葱，再加番茄略炒，最後加醬油及②料，放入麵及蝦仁一同炒拌均勻即成。

FRIED BROAD NOODLES WITH SHRIMP SERVES 2

	1 lb. (450 g.) cooked broad noodles
	1/2 lb. (225 g.) shrimp, shelled
①	1/2 T. cooking wine or sherry
	2 t. cornstarch
	1/4 t. salt
	1-1/2 c. onion, sliced in thin half circles
	1 c. tomato, cut in chunks
	2 T. soy sauce
	2 green onions, cut in 1-1/2" (4 cm) sections
	1/2 c. water
②	1-1/2 t. sugar
	1 t. cornstarch
	1/3 t. salt
	pinch of pepper

❶ Wash the shrimp, drain, and pat dry with paper towels. Marinate in ①.
❷ Heat 3 tablespoons oil in a preheated wok. Stir-fry the shrimp until done and remove. Heat another tablespoon of oil. Stir-fry the onion until fragrant, then add the tomato and stir-fry briefly. Add the soy sauce and ②, stir-fry, then put in the cooked noodles and shrimp. Stir-fry briefly until well combined and serve.

空心菜。
Kung-hsin tsai, also called
ung-choi (空心菜;蕹菜).

青菜的種類不限定，可用茼蒿菜，
青江菜、菠菜取代。
Use any leafy green vegetable,
such as bok choy or spinach.

沙茶醬是以花生油、花生粉、炸香
紅葱頭、香菜子、蒜頭粉、花椒、
八角、蝦米磨碎製成。
Chinese barbecue sauce (沙茶醬),
is made from peanut oil, peanut
powder, fried shallots, coriander
seeds, garlic powder, Szechuan
peppercorns, star anise, and dried
shrimp ground together.

沙茶牛肉炒麵 2人份

①	牛肉(切片)············150公克(4兩)	
	醬油、料酒 ··············	各½大匙
	太白粉 ················	
②	沙茶醬 ·················	1½大匙
	葱、薑末 ··············	各½大匙
	蒜末 ·················	½小匙
	青菜 ·················	225公克(6兩)
③	高湯或水 ···············	¾杯
	醬油 ·················	1大匙
	糖 ··················	½小匙
	塩 ··················	⅓小匙
	胡椒 ·················	少許
	乾麵 ·················	150公克(4兩)

❶半鍋水燒開，放入麵條，再燒開後改小火煮約4分鐘至熟撈出，加1大匙油略拌以免麵條黏在一起。

❷牛肉片加①料拌醃備用。油1大匙燒熱，放入青菜略炒盛出，瀝乾水份。再加油3大匙炒熟肉片鏟出，餘油炒香②料，加③料燒開，加麵、牛肉及青菜一同炒勻即成。

■乾麵也可用熟油麵450公克(12兩)來代替。

FRIED NOODLES WITH BEEF IN BARBECUE SAUCE SERVES 2

①	1/3 lb. (150 g.) beef, sliced
	1/2 T. each: soy sauce, cooking wine or sherry, cornstarch
②	1-1/2 T. Chinese barbecue sauce (沙茶醬)
	1/2 T. each: green onion, ginger root; both minced
	1/2 t. garlic, minced
	1/2 lb. (225 g.) leafy green vegetable of your choice, washed and cut
③	3/4 c. stock or water
	1 T. soy sauce
	1/2 t. sugar
	1/3 t. salt
	pinch of pepper
	1/3 lb. (150 g.) dry noodles

❶ Bring half a pot of water to a boil and put in the dry noodles. When the water comes to a second boil, lower the heat and cook until the noodles are done, about 4 minutes. Remove and drain. Mix in 1 tablespoon oil to prevent the noodles from sticking together.

❷ Heat 1 tablespoon oil in a preheated wok and stir-fry the leafy green vegetable briefly. Remove and drain. Heat another 3 tablespoons oil and stir-fry the beef slices until done. Remove. With the oil remaining in the wok, stir-fry ② until fragrant. Add ③ and bring to a boil. Put in the cooked noodles, beef and vegetable. Stir-fry together briefly until thoroughly combined. Serve.

■ 1 lb. (450 g.) of precooked noodles (油麵) may be substituted for the dry noodles.

油麵一般都是熟的，只在開水內燙
洗後即可使用。
Precooked noodles need only be
immersed briefly in boiling water
to prepare for use.

①料：豬肉、香菇、蝦米及韭菜白
色部份。
The ingredients of ①: pork, dried
Chinese black mushrooms, small
dried shrimp; and the white
portion of Chinese chives.

豆芽、韭菜。
Mung bean sprouts and Chinese
chives.

芽菜肉絲炒麵 2人份

	台式油麵··········	450公克(12兩)
	油·············	2大匙
①	豬肉(切絲)·········	150公克(4兩)
	香菇(泡軟、切絲)·····	2朵
	蝦米(泡水)········	1大匙
	韭菜白色部份·······	適量
	醬油···········	1大匙
	高湯或水·········	½杯
	醋············	½大匙
②	辣豆瓣醬·········	½小匙
	塩············	¼小匙
	胡椒···········	少許
	豆芽菜··········	2杯
	韭菜(切3公分長)·····	1杯
	紅蘿蔔(煮熟切絲)····	½杯

❶油麵放在開水內燙洗後撈出。

❷油2大匙燒熱，先將韭菜白色部份及①料炒香，再加醬油及②料燒沸，隨入油麵、豆芽菜及韭菜、紅蘿蔔拌炒均勻即成。

■如用乾麵來炒，需乾麵150公克(4兩)，煮過後變為3倍，放入冷水內漂洗後拌入1大匙油即可使用。

FRIED NOODLES WITH BEAN SPROUTS AND MEAT SHREDS SERVES 2

1 lb. (450 g.) precooked noodles
　(油麵)
2 T. oil

① 1/3 lb. (150 g.) pork, shredded
2 dried Chinese black
　mushrooms, soaked and cut
　in julienne strips
1 T. small dried shrimp, soaked

white portion of Chinese chives,
　as desired
1 T. soy sauce

② 1/2 c. stock or water
1/2 T. vinegar
1/2 t. hot bean paste
1/4 t. salt
pinch of pepper

2 c. mung bean sprouts
1 c. Chinese chives,
　cut in 1-1/4″ (3 cm) sections
1/2 c. carrot, cooked and
　cut in julienne strips

❶ Immerse the precooked noodles in boiling water briefly and remove.

❷ Heat 2 tablespoons oil in a preheated wok. Stir-fry the white portion of the Chinese chives and ① until fragrant. Add the soy sauce and ② and bring to a boil. Put in the precooked noodles, bean sprouts, Chinese chives, and carrot. Stir-fry briefly to combine the ingredients, and serve.

■ If you use dry noodles instead of precooked noodles, use 1/3 lb. (150 g.). They will triple in volume and weight after cooking. Immerse in a bowl of cold water after cooking, drain, and mix in 1 tablespoon oil before use.

各廠牌醬油鹹度不同，需酌量增減。
The saltiness of soy sauce varies from brand to brand. You may have to increase or decrease the amount used according to taste.

醬汁B內的芝麻醬可用花生醬取代。
Peanut butter may be substituted for the sesame paste in dressing B.

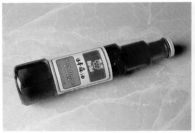

麻油味香，如無可用沙拉油取代。
Sesame oil adds a delicious aroma and taste to the dressing, but if unavailable, you may use regular cooking oil as a substitute.

鷄絲拌麵 2人份

鷄腿⋯⋯⋯⋯⋯2隻450公克（12兩）
乾麵⋯⋯⋯⋯⋯⋯⋯⋯150公克（4兩）
蛋⋯⋯⋯⋯⋯⋯⋯⋯⋯⋯⋯⋯ 2個
① { 小黃瓜⋯⋯⋯⋯⋯⋯⋯ } 均切絲
　 { 芹菜⋯⋯⋯⋯⋯⋯⋯⋯ } 共2杯
醬汁：
A { 醬油、麻油⋯⋯⋯⋯⋯⋯ 各2大匙
　 { 糖、醋⋯⋯⋯⋯⋯⋯⋯⋯ 各1大匙
或
B { 麻油、水⋯⋯⋯⋯⋯⋯ 各2½大匙
　 { 醬油、芝麻醬（或花生醬）‥各2大匙
　 { 糖、醋⋯⋯⋯⋯⋯⋯⋯ 各2小匙

❶鷄腿煮熟，撕成絲，麵煮熟冲冷水，瀝乾後加½大匙油拌勻（麵的煮法參考第6頁）。油1大匙燒熱，蛋打散放入炒至凝固盛出，或煎成蛋皮後切絲。

❷盤內盛麵，再擺適量鷄絲及①料，食時淋上醬汁A或B即可食。

■煮鷄腿時水份剛淹滿鷄腿即可，不要太多水煮出來的鷄腿較鮮。

■調醬汁B時，宜先將芝麻醬備碗內，再把其他佐料一一加入每次加入一種調勻後再加第二種，直至均勻爲止，否則易起顆粒。

■如喜食辣味可在醬汁內酌加辣油。如喜食熱麵，則麵煮後不冲冷水，直接淋上醬汁並拌料即可。

NOODLE SALAD WITH CHICKEN SHREDS SERVES 2

2 chicken legs (1 lb. or 450 g.)
1/3 lb. (150 g.) dry noodles
2 eggs
① { total of 2 c.:
　 { gherkin cucumber,
　 { celery; both shredded
Dressings:
A { 2 T. each: soy sauce, sesame oil
　 { 1 T. each: sugar, vinegar
　　　　　or
B { 2-1/2 T. each: sesame oil, water
　 { 2 T. each: soy sauce,
　 { 　 sesame paste
　 { 　 (or peanut butter)
　 { 2 t. each: sugar, vinegar

❶ Cook the chicken legs until done. Tear into shreds. Cook the noodles and rinse under cold running water. (See p. 6 for directions on how to cook noodles.) Drain and mix in 1/2 tablespoon oil. Heat 1 tablespoon oil in a preheated wok. Beat the eggs lightly and stir-fry until set. Remove. The egg may also be pan-fried into a pancake shape and shredded.

❷ Put a portion of cooked noodles in each serving dish. Top with chicken shreds and ①. Pour some of dressing A or B over the top and serve. Toss well before eating.

■ Use just enough water to cover the chicken legs when cooking for a fresher flavor.

■ When preparing dressing B, it is best to first put the sesame paste in a bowl, then add the other ingredients one by one in order. Mix each one thoroughly before adding the next. This will result in a smoother dressing without lumps.

■ If you like your noodles spicy-hot, add a little chili oil (辣油) to the dressing. If you prefer hot noodles, do not rinse the noodles under cold water. Put the salad ingredients directly on top of the hot noodles.

切洋葱時底部如不完全切斷就不會
散開。
Leave the bottom portion of the
onion intact while cutting to
prevent the onion from slipping
away and the pieces from
scattering.

橫過來切丁時比較容易。
Holding the onion sideways makes
it easier to cut.

豆瓣醬因廠牌不同，鹹度也有差別，
故需酌量增減使用份量。
The saltiness of bean paste varies
from brand to brand. Increase or
decrease quantity used according
to taste.

炸醬麵 2人份

絞肉‥‥‥‥‥‥‥‥‥‥225公克(6兩)
洋葱(切丁)‥‥‥‥‥‥‥‥‥‥‥ 1杯
豆瓣醬(或醬油)‥‥‥‥‥‥ 4大匙
① 水‥‥‥‥‥‥‥‥‥‥‥‥‥‥½杯
太白粉‥‥‥‥‥‥‥‥‥‥‥ 2小匙
麻油‥‥‥‥‥‥‥‥‥‥‥‥ 2小匙
糖‥‥‥‥‥‥‥‥‥‥‥‥‥ 1小匙
② 紅蘿蔔‥‥‥‥‥‥‥
小黃瓜‥‥‥‥‥‥‥ } 均切絲
生菜‥‥‥‥‥‥‥ 共3杯
乾麵‥‥‥‥‥‥‥‥‥‥150公克(4兩)
或新鮮麵‥‥‥‥‥‥‥225公克(6兩)

❶油5大匙燒熱,先炒香洋葱,入絞肉炒熟,隨入豆瓣醬炒香,再加①料燒開攪拌成濃稠狀即成炸醬。
❷半鍋水燒開,放入麵,改中火煮4分鐘,撈出分盛麵碗內(麵的煮法參考第6頁),上擺②料及炸醬,趁熱食用。
■喜愛蒜味者,可在煮好的炸醬內加些蒜末。

GROUND MEAT AND VEGETABLES WITH BEAN PASTE OVER NOODLES SERVES 2

1/2 lb. (225 g.) ground pork
  or beef
1 c. onion, cubed
4 T. bean paste (or soy sauce)
① 1/2 c. water
2 t. cornstarch
2 t. sesame oil
1 t. sugar
② total of 3 c.:
carrot,
gherkin cucumber,
lettuce, all shredded
1/3 lb. (150 g.) dry noodles or
  1/2 lb. (225 g.) fresh noodles

❶ Heat 5 tablespoons oil in a preheated wok. Stir-fry the onion until fragrant, then add the ground meat and stir-fry until cooked through. Add the bean paste and stir-fry until fragrant. Add ① and bring to a boil. Cook until a thick sauce forms. This is the meat and vegetable topping for the noodles.
❷ Bring half a pot of water to a boil, and put in the noodles. When it comes to a second boil, cook over medium heat until done, about 4 minutes. (See p. 6 for directions on how to cook noodles.) Remove noodles from water and put a portion in each serving bowl. Top each with some of ② and the topping, and serve hot. Mix well before eating.
■ If you like garlic, sprinkle a little fresh minced garlic over the meat and vegetable topping.

肉先調①料再拌入魚漿。
Marinate the meat in ① then add
to the fish paste.

如有現成炸香紅葱頭，做法❷內炒
香的步驟可省略。
If ready-fried shallots are used,
omit stir-frying in step ❷.

切好的筍絲罐頭用起來方便。
Sliced canned bamboo shoots
offer extra convenience.

肉粳麵線 ²人份

	豬或雞肉··············	112.5公克(3兩)
①	醬油、水················ 太白粉·················	} 各½大匙
	魚漿··················	112.5公克(3兩)
	紅葱頭或葱白(切薄片)···	1½大匙
	香菇(泡軟、切絲)··········	2朵
	醬油·················	1½大匙
	筍················· 紅蘿蔔···············	} 均切絲 共1杯
②	高湯或水···············	4杯
	糖··················	1小匙
	麻油、塩··············	各½小匙
	胡椒·················	少許
③	太白粉················ 水··················	3大匙 3大匙
	葱末、香菜·············	各2大匙
	麵線···············	120公克(3兩)

❶肉切片，加①料再加魚漿拌醃。

❷油2大匙燒熱，將紅葱頭及香菇炒香，加醬油1½大匙，隨加②料燒開，將肉片裹魚漿一片片加入，待燒開以③料勾芡，撒上葱末、香菜即成肉粳湯。

❸多量水燒開，入麵線煮熟撈出，分盛二個碗內，加入做好的肉粳湯，並酌加些黑醋及辣椒醬趁熱供食。

■此道爲家鄉口味，②料內的高湯如能以乾魷魚煮成湯使用，其味更佳。

■魚漿：將魚肉壓成泥狀，拌入調味料。或在中國魚店買現成的魚漿。

PORK AND FISH PASTE SOUP WITH VERMICELLI SERVES 2

	1/4 lb. (112.5 g.) pork or chicken
①	1/2 T. each: soy sauce, water, cornstarch
	1/4 lb. (112.5 g.) fish paste
	1-1/2 T. shallots (or white portion of green onion), thinly sliced
	2 dried Chinese black mushrooms, soaked and cut in julienne strips
	1-1/2 T. soy sauce
	total 1 c.: bamboo shoots, carrots; both shredded
②	4 c. stock or water
	1 t. sugar
	1/2 t. each: sesame oil, salt
	pinch of pepper
③	3 T. cornstarch
	3 T. water
	2 T. each: green onion, minced; fresh coriander, chopped
	1/4 lb. (120 g.) vermicelli (麵線)

❶ Slice the meat and marinate in ①. Mix in the fish paste.

❷ Heat 2 tablespoons oil in a preheated wok. Stir-fry the shallot and mushroom until fragrant. Add 1-1/2 tablespoons soy sauce, then ②, and bring to a boil. Add the meat slices in fish paste, one by one. When the liquid boils, add ③ to thicken. Sprinkle the minced green onion and the chopped fresh coriander over the top.

❸ Fill a pot half-full with water and bring to a boil. Put in the vermicelli; bring to a boil, then remove. Divide between two serving bowls. Pour the prepared soup over the top of each. Serve hot. A little Chinese black vinegar and chili paste can be added, optionally, for extra flavor.

■ This dish is native to Taiwan. Using stock produced by soaking dried cuttlefish for the soup stock in ② will enhance the flavor of this dish.

■ Fish paste: Debone a fish and press the flesh into a paste, seasoning to taste. Ready-made fish paste is available in Chinese fish shops.

蒜的兩端切去，再用刀拍破，則其皮易於去除。
Cut off the ends of the garlic clove, then smash with the side of a cleaver. The skin can now be easily removed.

九層塔是有特殊香味的蔬菜。
Fresh sweet basil leaves add a unique flavor.

如無九層塔就以香菜或青葱取代。
If fresh basil is unavailable, substitute fresh coriander leaves or chopped green onion.

蚵仔麵線 ^{2 人份}

	蚵	450公克 (12兩)
①	料酒	½ 大匙
	塩	⅙ 小匙
	太白粉	3 大匙
	蒜瓣 (拍破)	2 粒
	醬油	1½ 大匙
②	料酒	2 大匙
	高湯	4 杯
	塩、味精	各¼ 小匙
	胡椒	少許
	太白粉	1½ 大匙
	九層塔或香菜	1 杯
	麵線	120公克 (3兩)

❶蚵加塩水輕抓洗數次，放入開水內川燙，撈出瀝乾水份，加①料拌勻備用。

❷油２大匙燒熱，爆香蒜，加醬油及②料燒開成濃稠狀，隨入蚵及九層塔，即成蚵仔湯。

❸多量水燒開，入麵線煮熟撈出，分盛二個碗內，加入做好的蚵仔湯，並酌加黑醋及辣椒醬趁熱供食。

■麵線有多種，有些很容易爛，煮開立即撈出。

OYSTER SOUP WITH VERMICELLI SERVES 2

	1 lb. (450 g.) oysters, shelled
①	1/2 T. cooking wine or sherry
	1/6 t. salt
	3 T. cornstarch
	2 cloves garlic, smashed
	1-1/2 T. soy sauce
②	2 T. cooking wine or sherry
	4 c. stock
	1/4 t. salt
	pinch of pepper
	1-1/2 T. cornstarch
	1 c. fresh basil leaves or fresh coriander, chopped
	1/4 lb. (120 g.) vermicelli (麵線)

❶ Wash the oysters by rubbing gently in several changes of salt water. Blanch in boiling water. Remove and drain. Marinate in ① and set aside.

❷ Heat 2 tablespoons oil in a preheated wok. Stir-fry the garlic until fragrant, then add the soy sauce and ② and boil until a thick sauce forms. Stir in the oysters and fresh basil and remove from heat. This is the oyster soup.

❸ Bring a pot a little more than half-full of water to a boil. Cook the vermicelli until done and remove. Put half of the noodles in each of two serving bowls. Pour some of the oyster soup over each. Add a little Chinese black vinegar and chili paste for extra flavor. Serve hot.

■ There are many different kinds of vermicelli. Some cook very quickly and should be removed from the water as soon as it boils.

乾米粉需在開水內川燙一下，立即撈出備用。
Dry rice noodles must be immersed in boiling water for a few seconds, then removed immediately.

炒米粉或炒麵如用蝦米、香菇、洋葱先炒香，再拌入其他料，炒出來的米粉或麵，特別香。
Stir-frying small dried shrimp, dried black mushrooms, and onion until fragrant, then mixing in the other ingredients, results in especially tasty fried noodles or rice noodles.

放入的配料除包心菜與紅蘿蔔之外，也可用其他蔬菜。
Other vegetables can be substituted for the cabbage and carrot.

炒米粉 ^{2 人份}

乾米粉‥‥‥‥‥‥‥‥‥150公克（4兩）
前腿肉或五花肉（切絲）‥‥‥‥‥‥‥
　　‥‥‥‥‥‥‥‥‥150公克（4兩）
① ｛蝦米（泡水）‥‥‥‥‥‥‥‥2大匙
　 ｛香菇（泡軟，切絲）‥‥‥‥‥2朵
　 ｛洋蔥（切絲）‥‥‥‥‥‥‥‥1杯
醬油‥‥‥‥‥‥‥‥‥‥‥‥1½大匙
② ｛水或高湯‥‥‥‥‥‥‥‥‥‥1杯
　 ｛塩‥‥‥‥‥‥‥‥‥‥‥‥¼小匙
　 ｛胡椒‥‥‥‥‥‥‥‥‥‥‥少許
③ ｛包心菜（切絲）‥‥‥‥‥‥‥2杯
　 ｛紅蘿蔔（切絲）‥‥‥‥‥‥‥1杯

❶水燒開，米粉放入燙一下立即撈出，備用。
❷油4大匙燒熱，放入肉絲爆香，依序放入①料炒香，並加醬油略炒，加②料燒開，放入米粉及③料翻拌至汁全部收乾即成。

FRIED RICE NOODLES SERVES 2

1/3 lb. (150 g.) dry rice noodles
（米粉）
1/3 lb. (150 g.) pork, part fat,
　shredded
① ｛2 T. small dried shrimp, soaked
　 ｛2 dried Chinese black
　 ｛　mushrooms, soaked and cut in
　 ｛　julienne strips
　 ｛1 c. onion, sliced in half-circles,
　 ｛　rings separated
1-1/2 T. soy sauce
② ｛1 c. water or stock
　 ｛1/4 t. salt
　 ｛pinch of pepper
③ ｛2 c. cabbage, shredded
　 ｛1 c. carrot, shredded

❶ Bring a pot of water to a boil and immerse the dry rice noodles in it for a few seconds. Remove from the water and set aside.

❷ Heat 4 tablespoons oil in a preheated wok. Stir-fry the meat shreds, then add the ingredients in ① one by one in order. Add the soy sauce and stir-fry briefly. Add ② and bring to a boil. Put in the rice noodles and ③. Stir-fry until all the liquid has been absorbed. Serve hot.

河粉勿燙水，以免太爛不好吃。
Do not immerse the broad rice noodles in boiling water before frying, or they will become too mushy.

市面上有筍絲罐頭用來方便。
Buy ready-shredded canned bamboo shoots for extra convenience.

如無韭黃，可用韭菜取代。
If yellow Chinese chives are unavailable, substitute regular green Chinese chives.

炒河粉 2人份

河粉·················· 450公克 (12兩)
鷄、牛或豬肉 (切絲)150公克 (4兩)
① { 醬油、水··············
   太白粉·············· } 各½大匙
葱、薑末················· 各1大匙
② { 青椒 (切絲)··············½杯
   紅辣椒 (切絲)···········1大匙
③ { 高湯或水···············½杯
   醬油·················· 1½大匙
   塩·····················¼小匙
   胡椒··················少許
   筍絲··················· 1杯
   韮黃··················· 1杯

❶河粉切條。肉絲加①料拌勻備用。
❷油3大匙燒熱，放入肉絲炒至熟撈出。餘油炒葱、薑及②料，再加③料，放回肉絲一同燒開，放入河粉及韮黃炒拌均勻即成。

FRIED BROAD RICE NOODLES SERVES 2

1 lb. (450 g.) rice noodle sheets
  (河粉)
1/3 lb. (150 g.) chicken, beef,
  or pork, shredded
① { 1/2 T. each: soy sauce, water,
     cornstarch
   1 T. each: green onion,
     ginger root; both minced
② { 1/2 c. green pepper,
     cut in julienne strips
   1 T. hot red pepper, shredded
③ { 1/2 c. stock or water
   1-1/2 T. soy sauce
   1/4 t. salt
   pinch of pepper
   1 c. bamboo shoots, shredded
   1 c. yellow Chinese chives,
     cut in 1-1/4" (3 cm) sections

❶ Cut the rice noodle sheets into strips to make the broad rice noodles. Marinate the meat in ① and set aside.

❷ Heat 3 tablespoons oil in a preheated wok. Stir-fry the meat shreds until done and remove. With the oil remaining in the wok, stir-fry the green onion, ginger, and ② until fragrant. Add ③, and return the meat to the wok. Bring to a boil, then add the broad rice noodles and yellow Chinese chives. Stir-fry until all ingredients are well combined. Serve hot.

年糕如是整條的，先切片再燙水，
如是新鮮的則免燙。
If you are using unsliced New
Year's cake, slice first, then
immerse in boiling water. Fresh
New Year's cake need not be
immersed in boiling water.

配料無限制，小白菜、大白菜或其
他蔬菜均可用。
Any kind of vegetables may be
used in this dish.

③料內的葱白、香菇及蝦米均能增
加菜餚香味，如再加１大匙醬油味
更香。
The white portion of the green
onion, the dried black mushroom,
and the dried shrimp of ③ all add
rich flavor to this dish. An additional tablespoon of soy sauce
may be added for extra flavor.

炒年糕 ^{2人份}

	年糕·····················225公克（6兩）
①	大白菜··················300公克（8兩）
	紅蘿蔔（切絲）··················½杯
	瘦肉（牛、豬或鷄肉，切片）········
	·····················225公克（6兩）
②	醬油、料酒·············· } 各1大匙
	太白粉··············
③	葱白（切段）···············2枝
	香菇（切絲）···············2朶
	蝦米（泡水）···············2大匙
	醬油···················1大匙
④	葱葉（切段）···············2枝
	水·····················¼杯
	塩···················⅓小匙
	胡椒···················適量

❶年糕切片，瘦肉片加②料拌勻，炒前再拌入 1 大匙油則肉易炒散。

❷油 2 大匙燒熱，放入①料略炒軟盛出，瀝乾水。再加油 3 大匙炒熟肉片撈出，餘油炒香③料並加醬油及④料，最後加年糕，放回青菜及肉片一同炒拌至年糕熟軟即成，食時酌加辣豆瓣醬。

■冷凍切片年糕，只要在滾水內一燙，等年糕軟了不黏在一起即可撈出，漂冷水，再拌入½大匙油即可用。注意燙的時間不要過久，以免年糕太爛。

FRIED CHINESE NEW YEAR'S CAKE SERVES 2

	1/2 lb. (225 g.) Chinese New Year's cake (sticky cake made of glutinous rice flour)
①	2/3 lb. (300 g.) Chinese cabbage (Nappa)
	1/2 c. carrot, cut in julienne strips
	1/2 lb. (225 g.) lean pork, beef, or chicken, sliced 3/4" × 1-1/2" (2×4 cm)
②	1 T. each: soy sauce, cooking wine or sherry, cornstarch
③	2 green onions, white portion only, cut in 1-1/2" (4 cm) sections
	2 dried Chinese black mushrooms, soaked and cut in julienne strips
	2 T. small dried shrimp, soaked
	1 T. soy sauce
④	2 green onions, green part only, cut in 1-1/2" (4 cm) sections
	1/4 c. water
	1/3 t. salt
	pinch of pepper

❶ Slice the New Year's cake. Marinate the meat slices in ②. Mix in 1 tablespoon oil before stir-frying so the meat slices will separate easily.

❷ Heat 2 tablespoons oil in a preheated wok. Stir-fry ① briefly, until cooked soft. Remove and drain. Heat another 3 tablespoons oil and stir-fry the meat until done. Remove. With the oil remaining in the wok, stir-fry ③ until fragrant and add ④. Add the Chinese New Year's cake, and return the vegetables and meat to the wok. Stir-fry until the New Year's cake is cooked through and soft. Hot bean paste may be added before eating.

■Immerse frozen sliced New Year's cake in boiling water briefly, just long enough for it to soften and separate. Remove and immerse in cold water. Drain and mix in 1/2 tablespoon oil, and it is ready for use. Be careful not to leave the cake in the boiling water too long, or it will become mushy.

牛肉如能選有參雜些肥肉的，吃起
來比較嫩，也可加豬肝、蝦等。
Beef with fat marbling will be
more tender. Pork liver, shrimp,
etc., may also be used.

冬粉、魚丸、豆腐是火鍋中不可缺
少的材料。
Bean thread, fishballs, and bean
curd are indispensable ingredients
in Chinese hotpot.

白菜、金針菇、豆苗、綠色青菜如
茼蒿菜、菠菜、空心菜等均可使用。
Illustrated:
Chinese cabbage, golden
mushrooms, and peavine greens.
Other leafy green vegetables may
be substituted for the peavine
greens.

沙茶火鍋 4人份

① 牛肉(切薄片)··· 900公克(1斤8兩)
　高湯或水·····················9杯
　鹽··························1小匙
　番茄(切塊)··················1個
　葱段(切3公分長)··········12枝

② 豆腐························2塊
　魚丸·······················12粒
　冬粉(泡水略切)·············1把
　金針菇·············100公克(3兩)
　大白菜·············450公克(12兩)
　豆苗··············225公克(6兩)

沾料：

③ 蛋··························4個
　沙茶醬···················8大匙
　醬油·····················2大匙
　麻油、糖············各1大匙　拌
　辣椒醬、醋··········各1小匙　勻
　葱(切碎)···············4大匙
　蒜(切碎)···············1大匙
　薑(切碎)···············½大匙
　白飯······················4碗

❶①料燒沸，水若不夠時再補充，②料洗淨備在餐桌上，③料分盛在小碗內。

❷食用時依個人喜好，將②料及牛肉片等邊放入①料內煮熟，邊沾③料食用。

■牛肉片很薄，容易熟，故放入湯裏顏色一變即可食用。

■可準備麵或麵線，到最後時將麵放入燒煮，其味道鮮美。

■沙茶醬是以花生油、花生粉、炸香紅葱頭、香菜子、蒜頭粉、辣椒粉、花椒、八角、蝦米磨碎製成。

石頭火鍋：與沙茶火鍋大同小異，所不同的是先將鍋燒熱加麻油，放入蒜與洋葱炒香，續入牛肉炒熟盛出，加湯與各料燒開後，將牛肉放於中間，邊煮邊食。

HOTPOT WITH BARBECUE SAUCE SERVES 4

① 2 lb. (900 g.) beef, sliced very thinly
　9 c. stock or water
　1 t. salt
　1 tomato, cubed
　12 green onions,
　　cut in 1-1/4" (3 cm) sections

② 2 cakes bean curd
　12 fish balls
　1 bunch bean thread
　　(soaked and cut)
　3.5 oz. (100 g.) golden mushrooms
　　(金針菇)or any kind of mushrooms
　1 lb. (450 g.) Chinese cabbage
　　(Nappa)
　1/2 lb. (225 g.) peavine greens (豆苗)
　　or other leafy green vegetable
Dipping Sauce:

③ 4 eggs
　8 T. Chinese barbecue sauce (沙茶醬)
　2 T. soy sauce
　1 T. each: sesame oil, sugar
　1 t. each: chili paste, vinegar
　4 T. green onion, minced
　1 T. garlic, minced
　1/2 T. ginger root, minced
　4 c. cooked rice

❶ Bring ① to a boil. Add water if necessary. Wash ②, arrange on plates, and place on the dining table. Mix ③ thoroughly and put some in each serving bowl.

❷ Each person chooses his own ingredients of ② to cook at the table by immersing in ① until done. Use a chafing dish or electric wok. Dip in ③ before eating.

■ Thinly sliced beef will cook very quickly. Remove from the boiling stock as soon as it changes color.

■ Noodles or vermicelli may be cooked in the stock left after the ingredients of ② have been cooked in it and eaten. This stock is outstanding for noodles in broth.

■ Chinese barbecue sauce is made of peanut oil, peanut powder, fried shallots, coriander seeds, garlic powder, cayenne pepper, Szechuan peppercorns, star anise, and dried shrimp ground together.

Stone Hotpot

This dish is very similar to the above. The difference is that the pot is heated, sesame oil is added, and garlic and onion are stir-fried until fragrant. The beef is then stir-fried until just done, and removed. Next, the soup stock is added to the pot and brought to a boil. The beef is placed on the table with the other ingredients. Proceed as above.

前腿肉選略有肥肉參雜的為佳。
Choose pork taken from the foreleg with some fat on it for best results.

任何麵皮，均可用來包餡。
Use any type of flour wrapper.

味全公司出品燒烤醬味佳，除做叉燒肉外，可當郊遊烤肉用，非常方便。
Try Wei-chuan's Bar-B-Q Sauce for this recipe. It is also excellent for outdoor barbecues.

叉燒餡捲 6條份

	前腿肉	450公克（12兩）
	燒烤醬	4大匙
①	醬油、蠔油	¾大匙
	糖	2小匙
	水	¾杯
	太白粉	1大匙
②	蛋	6個
	塩	⅓小匙
	木須皮	6張

❶將肉切 1 ½吋寬長條，調燒烤醬拌醃數小時或醃隔夜使其入味更佳，燒烤時，先將烤箱燒熱至400°－450°再將肉放在烤盤上，放入中層烤40分鐘取出，切成約1公分四方薄片備用。
❷將①料盛入鍋內，燒開攪拌成濃汁，放入切好的叉燒肉片，另2大匙油燒熱，把②料打散，放入鍋內炒拌至凝固取出。
❸將木須皮攤開，放入適量的肉與蛋包捲而食。

BARBECUED PORK ROLLS 6 SERVINGS

1 lb. (450 g.) pork
(meat from forelegs)
4 T. barbecue sauce, any type
① 3/4 T. each: soy sauce,
oyster sauce
2 t. sugar
3/4 c. water
1 T. cornstarch
② 6 eggs
1/3 t. salt
6 Moo Shu shells
(Peking Duck flour wrappers)

❶ Cut the pork into strips, 1-1/2" (4 cm) wide. Marinate in the barbecue sauce for several hours or overnight so that the flavors are well absorbed. Preheat oven to 400°–450°F (205°–230°C). Put the pork in a baking pan and bake on the middle shelf for 40 minutes. Remove from oven and cut into thin slices 1/2" (1.25 cm) square.
❷ Put ① in a pot and bring to a boil. Cook until a thick sauce forms. Put in the sliced barbecued pork. Remove from heat. Heat 2 tablespoons oil in a preheated wok. Beat ② lightly and stir-fry until set. Remove.
❸ Roll some of the pork slices and egg in a moo shu shell and eat.

拌入炒熟芝麻特別香，但炒時火候不可太強以免燒焦。

The sesame seeds add a delicious, nutty flavor to this dish. Toast (use no oil) over low heat to prevent scorching.

包生菜、洋葱、紅蘿蔔、小黃瓜絲之外，包心菜、芹菜、酸菜均可任意選用。

Besides shredded lettuce, onion, carrot and gherkin cucumber; cabbage, celery and pickled mustard cabbage may also be used for ①.

炸好的餛飩皮裝入罐內可保存一、二星期不壞。

Leftover fried wonton skin strips can be kept in a container for one to two weeks.

生菜拌鷄絲 ²人份

鷄胸或鷄腿	450公克 (12兩)
①	包生菜(切絲)	3½杯
	洋葱、紅蘿蔔(切絲)	½杯
	小黃瓜(切絲)	1杯
	餛飩皮(切絲)	12張
	芝麻(炒熟)	1大匙
②	塩	½小匙
	醋	1½大匙
	糖	½大匙
	醬油、麻油	各1大匙

❶水(能滿過鷄即可)燒開後將鷄放入燒煮約20分鐘至肉熟取出待冷，除去骨，用手撕成絲或切粗條，②料調在碗內，餛飩皮切絲炸酥待用。

❷食時將鷄肉、①料、②料、餛飩皮、芝麻拌勻即成。

CHICKEN SHRED AND VEGETABLE SALAD SERVES 2

1 lb. (450 g.) chicken breast or leg meat

① 3-1/2 c. lettuce, shredded
total of 1/2 c.: onion, carrot; both shredded
1 c. gherkin cucumber, shredded

12 wonton skins, cut in strips
1 T. sesame seeds, toasted

② 1/2 t. salt
1-1/2 T. vinegar
1/2 T. sugar
1 T. each: soy sauce, sesame oil

❶ Bring a pot of water to a boil. Use just enough water to cover the chicken. Put in the chicken and cook until done, about 20 minutes. Remove and cool. Separate the meat from the bones. Tear into shreds by hand or use a cleaver to cut into strips. Mix ② in a bowl and set aside. Fry the wonton skin strips until golden and set aside.

❷ To eat, combine a portion of the chicken shreds, ①, ②, the fried wonton skin strips, and the sesame seeds.

將餡置中間，折成三角形。
Put a dab of filling in the center of the skin, then fold into a triangle.

由 1 公分處向前再折疊。
Fold again to a point about 1/3" from the ends.

由兩端沾水黏住。
Dip the ends in water to make them stick better and press firmly to seal shut.

餛飩湯 2人份

	絞肉	150公克 (4兩)
	蝦 (剁碎)	75公克 (2兩)
①	水	2大匙
	太白粉、料酒	各1大匙
	塩	½小匙
	麻油、胡椒	各少許
	餛飩皮	24張
②	高湯	4杯
	醬油	2小匙
	塩	½小匙
	麻油、胡椒	各¼小匙
③	香菇 (泡軟切片)	½杯
	紅蘿蔔片	½杯
	筍片	1杯
	豌豆莢 (燙熟)	½杯

❶將絞肉、蝦及①料拌勻成餡。餛飩皮中間放置一份餡，折成三角形，由1公分處向前再折疊，由兩端沾水黏住，共包24個。
❷②料燒開，放入③料再燒開，放入燙熟豌豆莢及煮熟餛飩，熄火，分盛碗內即成。
■煮餛飩：水燒開，放入餛飩再燒開，以中火煮4分鐘即成。如餡少皮薄，則燙煮的時間要縮短，餛飩皮的厚薄可依個人喜愛選用。

WONTON SOUP SERVES 2

- 1/3 lb. (150 g.) ground pork
- 2.6 oz. (75 g.) shrimp, shelled and chopped

①
- 2 T. water
- 1 T. each: cornstarch, cooking wine or sherry
- 1/2 t. salt
- few drops sesame oil
- pinch of pepper
- 24 wonton skins

②
- 4 c. stock
- 2 t. soy sauce
- 1/2 t. salt
- 1/4 t. each: sesame oil, pepper

③
- 1/2 c. dried Chinese black mushrooms, soaked and cut in thick strips
- 1/2 c. carrot, sliced
- 1 c. bamboo shoots, sliced
- 1/2 c. snow peas (Chinese peapods), blanched in boiling water

❶ Mix the ground pork, chopped shrimp, and ① together well to make the wonton filling. Put a dab of filling in the center of a wonton skin and fold over to form a triangle. Fold over again so the corners cross at a point about 1/3" (.75 cm) from the ends. Dip the ends in water and press together firmly. Wrap 24 wontons in this way.
❷ Bring ② to a boil in a pot. Add ③ and bring to a boil again. Put in the snow peas and boiled wontons. Turn off the heat, and ladle into serving bowls.

To Cook the Wontons:
Bring a pot of water to a boil. Put in the wontons and bring to a second boil. Cook 4 minutes over medium heat. If there is a small amount of filling in each wonton, and/or the skins are thin, cooking time will need to be reduced. Choose the wonton skin thickness you prefer when shopping.

令您賞心悅目的叢書

A SERIES OF BOOKS FOR YOUR PLEASURE AND ENJOYMENT

中國菜
- 180道菜
- 204頁
- 精裝本及平裝本
- 中文版、中英對照版

CHINESE CUISINE
- 180 recipes
- 204 pages
- paperbound edition
- Chinese, Chinese/English (bilingual) editions

中國菜實用專輯
- 89道菜附10道點心
- 104頁
- 平裝本
- 中文、英文及法文版

CHINESE COOKING FOR BEGINNERS
- 89 recipes and 10 snacks
- 104 pages
- paperbound edition
- Chinese, English and French editions

海鮮 專輯
- 161道菜
- 120頁
- 平裝本
- 中文版及英文版

CHINESE SEAFOOD
- 127 recipes
- 104 pages
- paperbound edition
- Chinese and English editions

簡餐專輯
- 47道簡餐
- 104頁
- 平裝本
- 中英對照版

CHINESE ONE DISH MEALS
- 47 recipes
- 104 pages
- paperbound edition
- Chinese/English (bilingual) edition

點心專輯
- 98道點心
- 100頁
- 平裝本
- 中英對照版

CHINESE SNA
- 98 snacks
- 100 pages
- paperbound ed
- Chinese/English (bilingual) editio

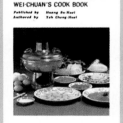

中國菜第二冊
- 187道菜附50種盤飾
- 280頁
- 精裝本
- 中英對照版

CHINESE CUISINE II
- 187 recipes and 50 garnishes
- 280 pages
- hardbound edition
- Chinese/English (bilingual) edition

愛與美插花
- 90種花藝
- 184頁
- 精裝本
- 中英對照版

MEDITATIONS ON NATURE
- 90 flower arrangements
- 184 pages
- hardbound edition
- Chinese/English (bilingual) edition

健康食譜
- 100道菜
- 120頁
- 平裝本
- 中英對照版

HEALTHFUL COOKING
- 100 recipes
- 120 pages
- paperbound edition
- Chinese/English (bilingual) edition

家常菜
- 226道菜
- 200頁
- 精裝本及平裝本
- 中文版

素食
- 84道菜
- 116頁
- 精裝本及平裝本
- 中英對照版

VEGETARIAN COOKING
- 84 recipes
- 116 pages
- paperbound ed
- Chinese/English (bilingual) editio

國立中央圖書館出版品預行編目資料

簡餐專輯＝Chinese one dish meals／黃淑惠
　編著．—初版．—臺北市：味全，民76
　　面：　公分
ISBN 957-9285-04-7(平裝)

1.食譜—速食

427.14　　　　　　　　　　　80000770

簡餐專輯
CHINESE ONE DISH MEALS

味全食譜　版權所有　　　局版台業字第0179號
　　　　　　　　　　　　台內著字第49990號

編著者：黃淑惠
發行者：黃淑惠
出版者：味全出版社有限公司
台北市仁愛路四段28號２樓
郵政劃撥0018203-8號黃淑惠帳戶
Wei-Chuan Publishing Co., Ltd.
2nd Fl., 28 Section 4, Jen-Ai Road,
Taipei, Taiwan
Tel: 702-1148~9　Fax: 7042729
美國總經銷：Wei-Chuan's Publishing
1455 Monterey Pass Rd., ＃110
Monterey Park, CA 91754, U.S. A
Tel: (213) 261-3880・261-3878
Fax: (213)261-3299

中華民國76年５月初版發行
中華民國80年４月６版發行

印刷：中華彩色印刷股份有限公司
地址：新店市寶橋路229號
定價：新台幣貳佰伍拾元整　　ISBN: 957-9285-04-7

COMMUNICATIVE AMERICAN ENGLISH

Grete Roland

National Textbook Company
NTC a division of *NTC Publishing Group* • Lincolnwood, Illinois USA

*This book is dedicated to the memory of Joan McClure
(formerly, Joan Hamm), a colleague, dear friend, and an indomitable
proponent of human rights. She would have enjoyed this book,
and she would have truly understood it.*

Cover Photos by Jeff Ellis

Published by National Textbook Company, a division of NTC Publishing Group,
© 1992 by NTC Publishing Group, 4255 West Touhy Avenue,
Lincolnwood (Chicago), Illinois 60646-1975 U.S.A.
Manufactured in the United States of America.
Library of Congress Catalog Card No. 91-60821

1 2 3 4 5 6 7 8 9 VP 9 8 7 6 5 4 3 2 1

Contents

Unit 5
The World of Work 65

Unit 6
In and Around the City 75

Unit 7
Cultural Differences and Reactions 91

Unit 8
Recreation, Vacation, and Sports 107

Unit 9
The Media 119

Unit 10
Politics 125

Acknowledgments

The author wishes to thank family and friends who have either mentioned or ferreted out animal-based expressions and shared them: my long-suffering husband, Kaz Mohan, for his contributions and for enduring my hours at the computer; my sister-in-law, Diane Roland; my dad, Arne Gulbrandsen; my son, Attila R. Salman; Leonore Nillisen; Sylvia Huie; and my colleagues Betsy Rubin, Rose DiGerlando, and Susan Doyle. I am also grateful to Richard A. Spears for his works, *NTC's American Idioms Dictionary* and *NTC's Dictionary of Slang and Colloquial Expressions*, which have been helpful resources. A special thanks to my editor, Kathleen Schultz, at National Textbook Company for her encouragement and gentle but wise suggestions for adjustments to the manuscript.

Introduction

To the Student

This book will help you gain both fluency in speaking American English and skill in understanding the English you hear on TV, on the radio, and in conversations at school, at work, and on the street. *Communicative American English* uses informal, sometimes colloquial, American English, the English that you will hear and want to use as you communicate in English.

When speaking, educated people commonly use the figurative expressions and idioms, including two- and three-word verbs, and the conversational phrases presented in the dialogues in this text. Even certain informal grammar that is not usually acceptable in written English is used by educated people on a regular basis in their speech. For example:

"Who is it?"
"It's *me*."

"It is *I*," the grammatically correct response, is considered pompous, or too formal, when used in spoken English. All the dialogues in this book are based on the speech of educated young adults and adults, not on how they write formally.

Many of the expressions in this book will not be appropriate for the papers in your high school or college English classes, since some of the expressions are considered clichés, expressions that are overused by native English writers. In such classes, more creative and sophisticated use of language is expected. Therefore, stick with the definitions and synonyms of the expressions found in the glossary at the end of this book instead. These definitions are written in formal language. However, you may use any of the expressions in this book when writing letters to friends, writing articles for newspapers and magazines, or in any other situation calling for conversational-style writing.

Communicative American English was written with you, the English language learner, in mind. When you listen to the dialogues, notice how a fluent speaker of English, your instructor, pronounces and "sings" the lines. Watch the nonverbal behavior: the facial expressions, the gestures, and the body movements. Human communication is complex and involves, besides the verbal elements that may have multiple meanings, an even greater number of nonverbal elements. Careful observation of native English speakers and frequent practice will help you to communicate more effectively in both verbal and nonverbal forms.

This book offers more dialogue units than can be covered in one semester, so that each instructor and class can "pick and choose" which ones to study. The ones you don't practice in class can be practiced with native-English-speaking friends outside of class. Have someone help you and strengthen a friendship at the same time! The glossary will also be useful to you in the real world of spoken American English outside the classroom. It contains an extensive collection of animal-based words and expressions, organized alphabetically by animal name. Using this textbook will acquaint you with the glossary in a short time, so you will be able to use it easily and acquire numerous expressions in the process.

Communicative American English will help you to build vocabulary and gain confidence in speaking English. Practice the dialogues out loud both in and out of class, preferably with a native English speaker or at least with another person. Also, do not stop there: initiate conversations and "small talk" with native or fluent English speakers on the topics covered in this text. When you hear unfamiliar words or expressions, you will be able to make intelligent guesses as to their meanings. Learning language does involve the unknown, as you have experienced already. Research has shown that people who learn languages fastest are those who can tolerate not knowing everything right away and who can use what they do know effectively. Try to develop this tolerance in addition to patience with yourself. Remember this old cliché: "Practice makes perfect." You may or may not achieve perfection (native speakers certainly do not), but practice, patience, and tolerance will certainly lead you to near-native fluency in American English. Good luck, and have fun with this living language and reference book!

To the Instructor

Communicative American English is a conversation and vocabulary text for students of American English at the intermediate and advanced college preparatory levels. High school students bent on improving their English as a second language (ESL) skills will find this book essential as it unlocks the mysteries of the vernacular for them. In fact, all youth and adults who are interacting within the American environment or who interact with Americans will greatly benefit from the cultural illuminations provided in this text through dialogues as well as through discussion, role-play, and group/partner activities.

The curriculum developer and the classroom teacher will find *Communicative American English* a suitable textbook for either a wholistic approach or for any of the traditionally segmented courses: conversation (listening and speaking), vocabulary and reading, and writing. For the latter course, it will facilitate comprehension and practice of both play writing and journalistic writing, the informal writing style used in newspapers and magazines. In fact, the choice of expressions presented in this book is based on their frequency of occurrence in newspapers, magazines, popular books, conversations, radio, television, and film.

The themes and titles of the units in this book are those commonly heard in conversation. Giving students the chance to discuss these topics will inevitably lead to language skill in other areas. The organization of the dialogue units by themes further facilitates a wholistic approach to second language learning. Since the book's definitions and explanations employ mostly formal language, they furnish the student with vocabulary for reading comprehension and for writing as well. In this way, the dialogue units and the glossary aid students in acquiring a larger vocabulary for both speaking and writing.

The figurative expressions used in the dialogues, which are often difficult to understand or find in the dictionary, are defined in the accompanying glossary, an extensive list of expressions, such as *for the birds* and *scapegoat,* based on animal words. The animal words serve as keys to numerous expressions. (Most of the expressions in this glossary adhere to the etymological origin of the animal; a few, however, may not, but are included because the animal associations will make the words and expressions memorable to students.) With this unique glossary, the book takes on the dual purpose of text and reference book. Most of the expressions and terms found in the glossary are used in the context of the dialogues, thereby achieving two major goals: contextual comprehension of conversational English and oral-aural practice. Speaking practice may take place through interaction with the instructor and through conversations with classmates in partnerships, role-playing, and group discussions.

The dialogues and discussions in the text include not only figurative expressions but also idioms, two- and three-word verbs, and proverbs. Since the glossary includes only expressions based on animal names, all other idioms, slang terms, and expressions are defined immediately following the dialogue in which they appear. In addition, a comprehensive list of these expressions and their definitions appears at the end of the book.

Many of the dialogues and much of the glossary have been field-tested in adult ESL classes by the author and her colleagues over a period of five years. The situations and exchanges included in the dialogues are based on actual occurrences and cultural settings found in the United States, so students relate to them well. Purposely, the text contains more material than can be covered in a semester of four fifty-minute class periods a week, so teachers have the option of choosing the dialogue lessons that will serve their classes best and with which they feel most comfortable. No doubt dialogues that are interesting or humorous to one teacher or class may not be so to another. Moreover, the dialogues may be studied in any order, since they are not sequenced in terms of language difficulty — although the dialogue topics become progressively more challenging.

Most of the dialogues contain cultural markers that will spur discussions on differences between various cultures. Moreover, an entire unit on cultural differences has been included. The dialogues and activities in this section treat subjects of frequent concern to people of minority cultures living in the United States. General class discussions and informal group discussions based on each lesson topic provide students with the opportunity to practice expressing their knowledge, opinions, and ideas. The whole process of learning figurative expressions, idioms, and slang enhances cross-cultural thinking and helps students cross over to natural, intelligible conversation in English. In addition to improving students' comprehension and use of vernacular American English, *Communicative American English* helps to lower the levels of student frustration that can be a significant barrier to finding fluency and fun in learning another language.

Key to Abbreviations

Here is a key to the abbreviations used throughout this book.

n.	(noun)
v.	(verb)
adj.	(adjective modifier)
adv.	(adverb modifier)
p/s	(proverb or saying)
tr.	(transitive)
in.	(intransitive)

Unit **1**
Family Relationships

Patty, My Sister

CAROL: My sister Patty is so childish.

SAM: Why do you say that?

CAROL: Well, first of all, she wears pigtails.

SAM: How old is she?

CAROL: She's sixteen, and she still bites her fingernails!

SAM: I see what you mean.

CAROL: Not only that, she lives high off the hog. So Mom finally told her to get a part-time job.

SAM: What was her reaction?

CAROL: Oh, she weaseled out of it as usual. And she wormed another ten dollars out of Mom.

Vocabulary Building

Check the glossary for the definitions of these terms:

➤ to live high off the hog (v.)

➤ pigtail (n.)

➤ to weasel out of (v.)

➤ to worm something out of someone (v.)

Write a synonym or synonymous phrase for each term in your notebook.

Questions

1. In what ways is Patty childish?

2. How are Patty and Carol related?

3. What does it mean to "live high off the hog"?

4. Why do you think Patty's mother told her to find work?

5. How did Patty react to her mother's suggestion?

6. How much money did Patty worm out of her mother?

Role Play

In groups of five, role-play the following situation.

Characters:

MOTHER   FATHER   OLDER BROTHER OR SISTER   YOUNGER BROTHER OR SISTER
GRANDPARENT

Situation:

The members of this family are meeting to discuss fair allowances and division of chores. The mother believes the older child should have more money than the younger one. The father believes both children should receive the same allowance. Of course, each of the children wants as much money as possible and has many reasons for needing money. The grandparent has his/her own opinion, but mainly wants the family to come to an agreement.

Discussion Topics

Childish Behavior: In your opinion, what is "childish behavior"? How should a person act at certain ages, such as ten, twenty, or thirty?

Being Responsible: In what ways have you learned to be responsible with money? Do you live according to your means or high off the hog? Explain your answer. Have you ever weaseled money out of your parents? If so, how did you do it? Do you earn money to pay for your own expenses? Why or why not?

Money Matters: What is your relationship to your family in regard to money? Do you find it difficult to afford the things you want? How will/do you provide money for your own children?

Bringing up Children: What is the best way to teach young people responsibility? Should young people get an allowance? If so, how much? Do the children in your family get an allowance? How did your parents teach you responsibility? Were the girls and boys in your family taught differently about responsibility? Explain your answers.

Baby-sitting

TOM: I have to look after my kid brother this week.

MARIA: Why is that?

TOM: My parents went out of town, so I'm stuck with him.

MARIA: That's not a very nice thing to say.

TOM: He apes everything I do. He's also a tattletale.

MARIA: I guess you'll have to behave yourself.

TOM: Right. I won't smoke or drink. Otherwise, it's monkey see, monkey do.

MARIA: It'll be good for you.

Vocabulary Building

Check the glossary for the definitions of these terms:

➤ to ape (v.)

➤ kid brother (n.)

➤ Monkey see, monkey do. (p/s)

Write a synonym or synonymous phrase for each term in your notebook.

Other Expressions

to look after   *to watch, to take care of*

stuck with someone or something   *burdened with someone or something*

tattletale   *one who tells other people's secrets*

Questions

1. How does Tom feel about looking after his brother?
2. What does Tom's brother do?

3. What is a **tattletale**? Is it good or bad? What condition might determine the use of this term?
4. How will Tom have to behave?
5. Why is it good for Tom to have his kid brother watching?
6. What do you think is Maria's opinion of Tom?

Role Play

In groups of four, role-play the following situation.

Characters:

TOM   TOM'S KID BROTHER (JEFF)   TWO OF TOM'S CLASSMATES

Situation:

Tom's kid brother Jeff, who is very spoiled, must go to a study session with Tom. Tom and two of his classmates planned this session in order to study for the final examination for their English course. While they are trying to practice their English, Tom's kid brother constantly demands attention. Tom tries to control Jeff, but his classmates gradually lose their patience.

Discussion Topics

Setting a Good Example: How do you set a good example for children and other young people? Do you think children learn best by imitating adults? What specifically could you do to be a good role model for the young people you know? Can adults be good role models for other adults? Explain your answer.

Choosing a Babysitter: If you were hiring a babysitter for your children, what kind of person would you choose? What criteria would you follow for your selection? How much would you pay the ideal babysitter?

The Holidays and In-Laws

HENRY: Why are you so down in the mouth?

JOHN: I've got a bear to solve.

HENRY: What's up?

JOHN: It's a problem with the holidays. Every year, we alternate spending Christmas and Thanksgiving at my mother's and my in-laws' homes.

HENRY: So what's the problem?

JOHN: My wife says my mother is always catty to her, so she refuses to go there for either holiday this year.

HENRY: Are you a man or a mouse? Show your wife who's top dog in the family.

JOHN: She wouldn't let me bully her.

HENRY: You sure are henpecked!

Vocabulary Building

Check the glossary for the definitions of these terms:

➤ Are you a man or a mouse? (p/s)

➤ bear (n.)

➤ to bully (v.)

➤ catty (adj.)

➤ henpecked (adj.)

➤ top dog (n.)

Write a synonym or synonymous phrase for each term in your notebook.

Another Expression

down in the mouth   *sad-faced, unsmiling*

Questions

1. Why is John down in the mouth?
2. Where does John spend Thanksgiving and Christmas?
3. How does John's mother behave toward her daughter-in-law?
4. What is John's wife's reaction to her mother-in-law?
5. Do you believe John is henpecked?
6. How could John show that he is top dog in the family?
7. Who is the top dog in your family? Why?
8. Does anyone bully you? Why or why not?

Role Play

In groups of four, role-play the following situation.

Characters:

THE COMPLAINER   THE HOG   THE PERPETUAL DIETER   THE DO-GOODER

Situation:

Four relatives are sharing a holiday dinner. They are sitting at a table that is beautifully decorated and filled with delicious dishes. One person in the family is the complainer; nothing seems good enough to him or her. Another relative always takes more helpings than the others. He or she is a hog. Another relative is always on a diet, but takes some of every dish served anyway. The fourth relative is a do-gooder, who tries to please everyone.

Discussion Topics

The Husband and Wife Relationship: In your opinion, who should make the decisions in a family? Who makes the decisions in your family? Does it depend on the situation? Who decides where your family will spend an important holiday? Does your family have a special way of making decisions together? If so, describe it.

The In-Laws: How could John solve the problem between his wife and his mother? Are you aware of a similar problem? How has it been solved? Have you had experience with any in-law problems? If so, describe one or two. Have they been solved? If not, how could they be solved?

Family Holidays: Where or with whom do you spend important holidays? What are some reasons people enjoy spending holidays with their families? What are some reasons people dislike spending holidays with their families? Marriage often changes a person's holiday traditions. What are some of the changes newlyweds experience?

Moving Out

ANDY: I can hardly wait until I can get my own apartment.

MATTIE: Why is that?

ANDY: I really need more space for myself. Our house is so crowded! Besides, my mother acts like a mother hen, and my father bullies all of us.

MATTIE: Don't let them cow you. Stick up for your rights.

ANDY: That's the trouble. I don't have any rights when I'm with them!

MATTIE: I know how you feel. My folks have a horse and buggy attitude about everything I want to do.

ANDY: That sounds familiar. My father insists that I be home before midnight.

MATTIE: Are you some kind of night owl?

ANDY: Not exactly. But once I start shooting the bull with my friends, I lose all sense of time.

MATTIE: Once you have your own place, you'll be free as a bird.

ANDY: As soon as I can keep the wolf from the door and support myself, I'll move out.

Vocabulary Building

Check the glossary for the definitions of these terms:

- ➤ to bully (v.)
- ➤ to cow (v.)
- ➤ free as a bird (adj.)
- ➤ horse and buggy (adj.)
- ➤ to keep the wolf from the door (v.)
- ➤ mother hen (n.)
- ➤ night owl (n.)
- ➤ to shoot the bull (v.)

Write a synonym or synonymous phrase for each term in your notebook.

Other Expressions

to move out   *to take one's belongings and leave a living or working place*

to stick up for   *to support*

Questions

1. Why does Andy want to get his own apartment?
2. Does Mattie offer any suggestions? If so, what are they?
3. Why does Mattie think Andy is a night owl?
4. Why does Andy sometimes stay out late?
5. What will happen when Andy gets a place of his own?
6. When will Andy move out?
7. Do you think Andy's plan to get his own place is a good one? Why or why not?

Role Play

In groups of five, role-play the following situation.

Characters:

ANDY   ANDY'S WIFE   ANDY'S MOTHER   ANDY'S FATHER

ANDY'S GRANDPARENT

Situation:

Andy is arriving for a visit at his parents' home with his new spouse. Andy met and married his wife while he was living away from home. His parents are old-fashioned and have lived most of their lives in a small town. His grandparent lives with them, too. Andy's wife is a sharp dresser from a big city. She is meeting and talking with Andy's family for the first time.

Discussion Topics

Freedom: If you live with your folks, how much freedom do you have? How much freedom would you like to have? Do your parents have a horse and buggy attitude? If so, in what way(s)? Share and discuss cultural differences concerning freedom and discipline for children of various ages.

Living on Your Own: Is it a good idea to live on your own if you can? At what age (if any) do you think people should move away from their parents? Is this age the same for males and females? Share and discuss cultural differences in attitudes and behavior toward being independent.

Unit 2

Making Friends and Getting Together

A Hot Summer

JOAN: Another hot day like this, and I'm finished.

MAT: In the dog days of summer, it's a good idea to go to the beach.

JOAN: You won't believe this, but I have to help a friend move.

MAT: That puts a monkey wrench in my plans. I thought you had the afternoon off.

JOAN: I'm sorry. My friend's been hounding me to do this for a month.

MAT: All right, it's your funeral! I'll go to the beach alone.

Vocabulary Building

Check the glossary for the definitions of these terms:

➤ dog days (n.)

➤ to hound (v.)

➤ monkey wrench (n.)

Write a synonym or synonymous phrase for each term in your notebook.

Other Expressions

to be finished *to be dead*
to have time off *to be free, especially to be free from work*
It's your funeral! *If you do it, you will suffer all the consequences.*

Questions

1. What kind of summer has it been?
2. What does Mat want to do?

3. Why does Joan turn down the suggestion to go to the beach?

4. Why is Mat disappointed?

5. How long has Joan's friend been hounding her to help with moving?

6. What is Mat going to do?

Role Play

In groups of two, role-play the following situation.

Characters:

THE MOVER   THE EVADER

Situation:

One person has to move and wants the other person to help. However, the second person is not very enthusiastic. The "mover" tries to persuade his or her friend to help, while the "evader" tries to make excuses for not helping.

Discussion Topics

Coping with the Heat: How do you cope with the dog days of summer? What do you wear? What kinds of food do you eat? Where do you go? Do you try to avoid certain kinds of activities? If so, which ones?

Moving: How often have you moved? Give some reasons why people move. What was the worst part of moving for you? What was the best part? What tips can you give on moving? In what ways can you make moving easier on yourself? How can the weather affect your moving plans?

The Dance

MARIO: Cat got your tongue? You're awfully quiet.

HELEN: Oh, hi, Mario! Thank you for inviting me to the party.

MARIO: I hope you're having a good time.

HELEN: Oh, I am. I'm always like a clam at first.

MARIO: Maybe you'll loosen up when everyone starts to dance.

HELEN: I'm a mean dancer once I get started.

MARIO: Then let's dance!

(pause)

HELEN: Do you think we're hogging the floor?

MARIO: Don't worry about it. You're terrific!

HELEN: You're not so bad yourself.

Vocabulary Building

Check the glossary for the definitions of these terms:

➤ to be like a clam (v.)

➤ Cat got your tongue? (p/s)

➤ to hog (v.)

Write a synonym or synonymous phrase for each term in your notebook.

Other Expressions

to loosen up   *to become relaxed*
mean dancer   *a very good dancer*

Questions

1. How did Helen act at the beginning of the party?
2. Do you think Helen was having a good time? Why or why not?
3. Who is a mean dancer?
4. What did Mario suggest?
5. What did Helen worry about?
6. How did Mario flatter Helen?
7. How did Helen flatter Mario?

Role Play

In groups of two, role-play the following situation.

Characters:

MARIO   HELEN

Situation:

A few days after the party, Mario and Helen run into each other (meet by accident). They exchange greetings and make "small talk." Choose from these "small-talk" topics: the weather, the party, mutual friends, school or work, travel in the city or on vacation, sports and recreational activities, and places to go and things to do for entertainment (movies, dances, restaurants, etc.).

Discussion Topics

The Perfect Host or Hostess: Describe a perfect host or hostess. When you have a party, what can you do to make your guests happy? How do you treat the shy ones?

Flattery: Some people say that "Flattery will get you anywhere." Discuss this old saying and give your views on flattery. Do you like to be flattered? Why or why not?

Going Shopping

CHRIS: How much did you pay for your new shoes? They're really sharp.

PAT: I bought them on sale for about twenty dollars.

CHRIS: Are they real leather?

PAT: As a matter of fact, they are. They go with my new outfit.

CHRIS: You certainly are a smart dresser.

PAT: I guess I'm sort of a clotheshorse. I like to look my best.

CHRIS: I'm always beavering away at working and studying, so I can't even shop for something decent to wear.

PAT: That's too bad. Any time you want to go shopping with me, I'd be glad to help you.

CHRIS: That's the best offer I've had in a long time.

PAT: You'll go ape over some of the stores I've found. But we should go when they have their sales.

CHRIS: Great! Then we can put on the dog together.

Vocabulary Building

Check the glossary for the definitions of these terms:

➤ to beaver away (v.)   ➤ to go ape over (v.)

➤ clotheshorse (n.)   ➤ to put on the dog (v.)

Write a synonym or synonymous phrase for each term in your notebook.

Other Expressions

to go with *to match in color and style*
sharp *fashionable or attractive*

Questions

1. What did Chris notice about Pat?
2. How much did Pat pay for the shoes?
3. What are the shoes made of?
4. When did Pat say they should go shopping?
5. What did Pat say about the stores?
6. What did Chris say they could do after shopping together?
7. Why doesn't Chris go shopping very often?

Role Play

In groups of three, role-play the following situation.

Characters:

CHRIS   PAT   SALESPERSON

Situation:

Chris and Pat are shopping together for fall and winter clothes. They enter one of Pat's favorite stores and are met by a salesperson who tries to help them. Pat finds many things to buy, but Chris isn't very enthusiastic about the store.

Discussion Topics

Shopping for Sales: What is the best way to shop for clothes? When is the best time to look for bargains? Where do you like to shop for clothes? Is it important to you to be fashionable? Why or why not? How can a person be fashionable without spending a lot of money?

Changing Styles: How do people's styles differ? Consider age, occasion, and situation. What were the styles for hair, makeup, and clothes when your parents were young? In your lifetime so far, how have styles changed? How would you describe *your* individual style? Do you know anyone who has a very distinctive style, *not* one promoted by popular fashion magazines?

A Sick Friend

JOHN: The doctor must have given me snake oil. I can't shake this cold.

CHRIS: You look flushed. Do you have a fever?

JOHN: I think so.

CHRIS: It's no wonder. The way you carry on, you make yourself a sitting duck for any bug.

JOHN: I know, I'm a party animal. Do you expect me to hibernate?

CHRIS: No way! You couldn't be sensible if you tried.

JOHN: Is this how you treat a dying friend?

CHRIS: What a chameleon! Come on, buck up. I'm sure you'll feel better soon.

Vocabulary Building

Check the glossary for the definitions of these terms:

- to buck up (v.)
- bug (n.)
- chameleon (n.)
- party animal (n.)
- sitting duck (n.)
- snake oil (n.)

Write a synonym or synonymous phrase for each term in your notebook.

Other Expressions

to carry on   *to behave in a foolish, excited, or improper manner*

No way!   *Absolutely not.*

no wonder   *not surprising*

to shake   *to get rid of*

Questions

1. What does John think about his doctor?

2. What kind of sickness does John have?

3. Is Chris surprised that John is sick? Why or why not?

4. What does Chris mean by "the way you carry on"?

5. Do you think John is willing to change his lifestyle?

6. Why does John say that he is a "party animal"?

7. How does John try to get sympathy from Chris?

8. Does Chris think John is dying?

Role Play

In groups of four, role-play the following situation.

Characters:

PATIENT   RECEPTIONIST   NURSE   DOCTOR

Situation:

A patient enters the doctor's office and tells the receptionist his or her name and appointment time. They exchange information; then the patient waits a short time. The nurse calls for the patient and takes him or her to an examining room. The nurse wants to know the reason for the visit and asks other questions. Finally, the doctor enters and the patient and doctor discuss the patient's symptoms and concerns. The doctor tells the patient what treatment and/or medicine is needed to solve the problem.

Discussion Topics

Partying: How do you have a good time? What kinds of parties do you enjoy? What do you like to do at parties? When you have a party, whom do you like to invite? What do you serve? When is the right time to leave a party?

Staying Healthy: What habits do you have that help you stay healthy? Do you have any habits that might cause you to get sick? If so, what are they? What could you do to change them?

Going Out

CAROL: Look at you! You've certainly put on the dog.

JODY: I'm going to see the elephant tonight.

CAROL: I hope you won't see pink elephants.

JODY: Don't worry. Last time I drank like a fish, and I lived to regret it.

CAROL: What happened to you?

JODY: Fortunately, nothing serious. But the next morning I had nothing to crow about. In fact, I felt sick and crabby the whole day.

CAROL: Where are you going tonight?

JODY: First I'm joining some friends at an art show. From there, a couple of us are bound for the theater. Afterwards, we might go dancing.

CAROL: I'm glad you learned your lesson about drinking.

JODY: Absolutely. I won't overindulge again.

CAROL: Have a good time, and watch out for the wolves.

Vocabulary Building

Check the glossary for the definitions of these terms:

➤ crabby (adj.)

➤ to crow (v.)

➤ to drink like a fish (v.)

➤ pink elephants (n.)

➤ to put on the dog (v.)

➤ to see the elephant (v.)

➤ to watch out for the wolves (v.)

Write a synonym or synonymous phrase for each term in your notebook.

Other Expressions

to live to regret something   *to suffer the consequences of one's actions*

bound for   *on the way to; planning to go to*

to learn one's lesson   *to learn something from experience; to learn something the hard way*

Questions

1. How does Jody look?
2. Where is she going?
3. How much did Jody drink the last time she went out?
4. Did anything happen to her?
5. How did Jody feel the next morning?
6. What are Jody's plans for tonight?
7. What is Carol happy about?
8. What advice does Carol give Jody?

Role Play

In groups of three, role-play the following situation.

Characters:

CAROL   JODY   SAM

Situation:

Carol, Jody, and Sam are planning a party to celebrate another friend's new job. Sam wants to serve alcohol at the party, but Carol and Jody don't like the idea. They give several reasons for not serving alcohol, and Sam gives some reasons for serving it. The friends must reach a decision about what to do.

Discussion Topics

Having a Good Time: What do you do to have a good time? Where do you go? What do you wear? Plan an evening with friends. Choose what you want to do, and estimate what the activities will cost each person. Then get into groups and describe the plans you've made. After all the group members have shared their plans, take a vote on the best way to spend an evening from the suggestions in your group.

A Social Problem: A social problem of serious concern in the United States is teenage and underage drinking. How would you solve the problems such as noise, vandalism, and driving accidents that arise when young people overindulge in alcoholic beverages at parties? Among other considerations, discuss appropriate roles for parents and other adults who can influence young people, alternate ways of having a good time, and the law.

Going to a Rehearsal

BARRY: Why are you wearing all that makeup?

JOSIE: I'm made up for a play. We're rehearsing today.

BARRY: Can I come and watch?

JOSIE: Sure. Come along. Just don't drive your pigs to market.

BARRY: Don't worry, I love the theater. What's the play about?

JOSIE: Some fat cat's family is going to the dogs.

BARRY: It sounds like a Tennessee Williams play.

JOSIE: As a matter of fact, you're right! It's *Cat on a Hot Tin Roof.*

BARRY: Wow! I saw the movie with Elizabeth Taylor twice.

JOSIE: If you're still interested, let's go.

BARRY: I wouldn't miss seeing you in that play for the world.

Vocabulary Building

Check the glossary for the definitions of these terms:

➤ busy as a cat on a hot tin roof (adj.)

➤ to drive one's pigs to market (v.)

➤ fat cat (n.)

➤ to go to the dogs (v.)

Write a synonym or synonymous phrase for each term in your notebook.

Other Expressions

to be made up *to be wearing a lot of makeup or cosmetics*

Come along. *Come with me.*

not for the world *not for anything (no matter what its value)*

Questions

1. What does Barry notice about Josie?

2. Why is Josie wearing so much makeup?

3. What is Josie afraid that Barry will do?

4. What is the play about?

5. Who wrote the play?

6. What does the title of the play mean?

7. How does Barry feel about seeing Josie in the play?

Role Play

In groups of three, role-play the following situation.

Characters:

JOSIE   BARRY   THE DIRECTOR

Situation:

Barry is "discovered" at Josie's rehearsal. Josie introduces Barry to the director of the play. The director likes Barry's voice and appearance and tries to convince him to be the lead actor's stand-in, just in case of accident or illness. Barry is flattered by the director's request, but he has stage fright and doesn't want to get involved.

Discussion Topics

The Theater: What plays have you read? What plays have you seen? Divide the class into groups and let each group member give a short description of a play. Decide in your group which description makes you most want to see that play. Why does the play sound interesting? If you haven't seen or read a play lately, tell about a movie you've seen or a book you've read.

Makeup: What are your opinions about the use of makeup? Who do you think should wear makeup, and when? How much makeup is "too much"? Do you think it's acceptable for women not to wear makeup? Why or why not? Compare and contrast the views of various cultures regarding makeup.

Unit 3

Romantic Intentions

A Good Time

HENRY: You looked like a fox in a hen house last night.

SAM: It was a great party. But the woman I'd like to see again wasn't interested in me.

HENRY: That sounds like a lot of bull.

SAM: No, it's true. I've been trying to ferret out some information about her all day.

HENRY: Which woman are you talking about?

SAM: Sandra Blake.

HENRY: You're kidding! She's my sister.

SAM: This is too good to be true. Can you arrange a meeting?

HENRY: I don't know. She's usually on her high horse. I've never tried to fix her up with anyone.

SAM: Tell her there'll be no one in my life except her from now on.

HENRY: I'll also tell her what a peacock you are.

Vocabulary Building

Check the glossary for the definitions of these terms:

➤ bull (n.)

➤ to ferret out (v.)

➤ fox in a hen house (n.)

➤ to get/be on one's high horse (v.)

➤ peacock (n.)

➤ You're kidding! (p/s)

Write a synonym or synonymous phrase for each term in your notebook.

Other Expressions

to fix someone up *to make a match; to bring together two people who might become romantically involved*

from now on *starting today and lasting forever*

Questions

1. What is Henry's opinion of Sam?
2. Why wasn't Sam completely happy about the party?
3. Who was the woman he wanted to see again?
4. Why did Sam become happy after talking to his friend?
5. What is Henry's sister like?
6. What does Sam want Sandra to know? Do you think he's telling the truth?
7. What does Henry call Sam? Why?

Role Play

In groups of three, role-play the following situation.

Characters:

HENRY   SANDRA   SAM

Situation:

Henry and his sister Sandra are walking through the park. Henry asks his sister what she thinks of Sam and tells her that Sam is interested in her. While they're talking about this subject, Sam comes by and joins them as they walk and talk.

Discussion Topics

Matchmaking: Have you ever played matchmaker? Have you fixed up a sister, brother, relative, or friend with anyone? Is it a good idea to do this? Have you ever been fixed up with someone? If so, was the match a success? Is matchmaking common in your culture? If so, who makes the matches? Are the matches usually successful?

The Blind Date: Have you ever gone on a blind date? If so, explain how it happened and what it was like. What do you think of this American custom? Are blind dates common in your native country? If you were to go on a blind date, what requirements would you make about your date?

A Hopeful Suitor

JOSIE: Have you seen Philip?

ANN: No, and I hope I never do!

JOSIE: What's bugging you?

ANN: I can't stand the way he dogs me. He turns up everywhere I go.

JOSIE: Don't forget he gave you a nice present for your birthday.

ANN: I hate to look a gift horse in the mouth, but he won't stop badgering me.

JOSIE: Have a heart! He's bats about you.

ANN: That's the trouble. I'm not ready to get hogtied yet.

Vocabulary Building

Check the glossary for the definitions of these terms:

➤ to badger (v.)

➤ bats (adj.)

➤ to bug (v.)

➤ to dog (v.)

➤ Don't look a gift horse in the mouth. (p/s)

➤ hogtied (adj.)

Write a synonym or synonymous phrase for each term in your notebook.

Other Expressions

can't stand   *can't tolerate*

to have a heart   *to be kind and generous*

to turn up   *to appear*

Questions:

1. Who is looking for Philip?

2. Why doesn't Ann want to see Philip?

3. What has Philip been doing?

4. Why does Josie think Ann should be nice to Philip?

5. Whom does Josie sympathize with? Why?

6. In your opinion, why doesn't Ann want to get hogtied?

Role Play

In groups of two, role-play the following situation.

Characters:

PHILIP   JOSIE

Situation:

Josie sees and talks to Philip at a local store. They leave the store and continue their conversation as they walk down the street. Josie likes Philip and wants him to stop making a fool of himself over Ann. Philip respects Josie's advice and realizes his approach with Ann has been wrong. The two friends also discuss Philip's future plans in the area of romance.

Discussion Topics

The Brush Off: How do you discourage someone from pursuing you? Is it wise of Philip to be persistent? Should he try some other approach? Should he play "hard to get"? If you were really interested in someone, how would you approach that person? Does it make a difference if you're male or female? Does age make a difference?

Early Marriage: In your opinion, what is the right age for marriage? Why? When did your parents get married? When did you marry, or when do you plan to marry? What kind of preparation does a person need for marriage (if any)?

Staying Single: How do you view bachelors (unmarried men)? How do you view bachelorettes (unmarried women)? Are you aware of any customs regarding single men and single women? If so, explain them. How do/would you feel about being a bachelor or a bachelorette?

The Con Artist

CON ARTIST: You look new. Have I seen you someplace before?

NEW STUDENT: I'm going to school here.

CON ARTIST: Where do you come from?

NEW STUDENT: I'm from France. I've only been here for three months.

CON ARTIST: Let me take you under my wing. I have connections.

NEW STUDENT: What? I don't understand.

CON ARTIST: You're just a fish out of water. You need someone like me to show you the ropes.

NEW STUDENT: Could you explain that to me, please?

CON ARTIST: Sure. Stick with me, kid. I'll keep the wolves from your door.

Vocabulary Building

Check the glossary for the definitions of these terms:

➤ a fish out of water (n.)

➤ to keep the wolves from the door (v.)

➤ kid (n.)

Write a synonym or synonymous phrase for each term in your notebook.

Other Expressions

con artist   *someone who makes a living by swindling people*

to have connections   *to have friends in important positions*

to show someone the ropes   *to share one's knowledge and experience with someone else*

to stick with   *to stay with; to stay close to*

to take someone under one's wing   *to protect and guide someone*

Questions

1. What does the con artist want to do with the new student?
2. How does the con artist try to win the new student's confidence?
3. What kind of connections do you think the con artist has?
4. What does the con artist think about the new student?
5. Why does the con artist call the new student "kid"?
6. How does the new student react to the con artist?
7. Do you think the con artist is male or female? Why?
8. Do you think the new student is male or female? Why?

Role Play

In groups of three, role-play the following situation.

Characters:

CARLA   SYLVIA   HARVEY

Situation:

Harvey is giving Carla, a new employee, his expert advice about their company, especially about whom to be friendly with and whom to avoid. He's trying to take Carla under his wing. Just as Harvey thinks he is succeeding with the young and gullible Carla, Sylvia, another employee, arrives on the scene. Sylvia is very sarcastic toward Harvey. She takes Carla with her and gives Carla some friendly advice.

Discussion Topics

Keeping the Wolves from the Door: Have you ever met a con artist? If so, what happened? How do you handle a smooth-talking person? What is the difference between a woman conning a man and a man conning a woman? How would you protect your sister, brother, or friend from a con artist?

Using Lines: Do men or women in your culture use "lines" (phrases or sentences meant to impress and interest the opposite sex)? What American lines have you heard? Translate/interpret a few lines you know or have heard. Do you think lines are a good way to attract members of the opposite sex? Why or why not? What are some alternatives to using lines?

The Engagement

TARA: Hi, Bob. Congratulations on your engagement to Harriet.

BARBARA: What? You didn't tell me you were engaged!

TARA: Oops! I guess I let the cat out of the bag.

BOB: It's too late now. I'm sorry, Barbara; I didn't know how to tell you.

BARBARA: I thought you were interested in me. Why have you been leading me on?

BOB: Wait a minute! You're the one who's been dogging me.

TARA: Oh, dear. I didn't mean to put a fly in the ointment.

BARBARA: Don't be cute. This fly-by-night friend of yours is a real two-timer.

TARA: This is where I duck out.

BOB: Go ahead, you stool pigeon.

Vocabulary Building

Check the glossary for the definitions of these terms:

➤ to dog (v.)

➤ to duck out (v.)

➤ fly-by-night (adj.)

➤ a fly in the ointment (n.)

➤ to let the cat out of the bag (v.)

➤ stool pigeon (n.)

Write a synonym or synonymous phrase for each term in your notebook.

Other Expressions

Don't be cute. *Don't try to be clever.*

to lead someone on *to falsely encourage a person's affections*

two-timer *a person who deceives a boyfriend or girlfriend by secretly going out with another person for romantic reasons*

Questions

1. Did Tara mean to let the cat out of the bag?

2. What did Bob do wrong?

3. What kind of person do you think Bob is?

4. How did Barbara feel after hearing about Bob's engagement?

5. What did Barbara call Bob? Do you think her reaction was justified?

6. Who was pursuing whom, according to Bob?

7. Who was pursuing whom, according to Barbara?

8. Did Tara help or hinder the situation?

9. Should Bob have called Tara a stool pigeon? Why or why not?

Role Play

In groups of three, role-play the following situation.

Characters:

BOB   HARRIET   A BUSYBODY

Situation:

At a party, the busybody tells Harriet about her fiance Bob's relationship with Barbara. When Bob arrives, he gets a cold reception from Harriet, who finally tells him what she has heard. Bob has some explaining to do.

Discussion Topics

Loyalty: Is loyalty important in a relationship? If so, how should one show loyalty? What is a reasonable balance between possessiveness and loyalty in a romantic relationship? What would you have done or said if you had been in Barbara's situation? Do you think Bob's behavior was right or wrong?

Interfering: Tara innocently became involved in Bob's "affairs." Is it proper to interfere in someone else's personal business? What matters do you consider "personal and private"? In what ways do people become involved in the romantic affairs of others on purpose? How do you react when someone deliberately interferes in your personal business? Give an example.

Getting Acquainted

TOM: Do you mind if I sit with you ladies?

JANE: It's OK with me.

MATTIE: Me, too.

TOM: *(to Jane)* I hope you don't think I'm pushy, but you're very attractive.

JANE: It's nice of you to say that. Do you come to this cafeteria often?

TOM: Once in a while. I noticed you the other day, and I wanted to meet you then. I love your hairdo.

JANE: Thanks. It's called a beehive. Maybe it's old-fashioned, but it keeps the hair away from my face. I don't wear it this way all the time.

TOM: It's neat. Well, I have to leave, but I hope to see you again soon. Bye.

JANE: Bye. *(to Mattie)* Wow! I can't believe he wanted to meet me. I'm so mousy, and I've got these ugly buckteeth.

MATTIE: Now maybe you'll believe me. I told you you're not bad-looking!

Vocabulary Building

Check the glossary for the definitions of these terms:

➤ beehive (n.)

➤ bucktooth (n.)

➤ mousy (adj.)

Write a synonym or synonymous phrase for each term in your notebook.

Other Expressions

to mind   *to dislike; to be against*

neat   *great; excellent*

pushy   *overly bold*

Questions

1. Do you think Tom was pushy?
2. How did Jane react to Tom's flattery?
3. What did Tom like about Jane?
4. Why does Jane wear her hair in a beehive?
5. Do you think Jane liked Tom? Why or why not?
6. Why was Jane surprised that Tom wanted to meet her?

Role Play

In groups of three, role-play the following situation.

Characters:

GEORGE   SARAH   JOANNE (SARAH'S FRIEND)

Situation:

George is interested in having a friendship with Sarah. However, Sarah has an inferiority complex, so every time George compliments her, she makes some negative comment about herself. Sarah's friend Joanne, on the other hand, contradicts her every line and gives examples to show how wonderful Sarah is. Their conversation continues with George paying a compliment, Sarah refusing it, and Joanne contradicting Sarah. Create a surprise ending!

Discussion Topics

Beauty: Is beauty "in the eye of the beholder"? What characteristics do you consider attractive? Do you think women have a different measure of beauty for other women than men have? Do you think men have a different measure of handsomeness for other men than women have? What are some advantages and disadvantages of being attractive and of being unattractive?

Meeting People: Where do you go if you want to meet new people, especially members of the opposite sex? What are some good places to meet people? What are some places you wouldn't try to meet people? What would you do if you saw a man or a woman you wanted to meet?

Unit 4

Being a Student

Cutting Class

JOAN: Oh, I just ducked the teacher. That was a close call!

STEVE: You must feel guilty about something.

JOAN: You're right. I cut his class today.

STEVE: Don't think you can outfox him. He wasn't born yesterday, you know.

JOAN: If he asks me why I missed class, I'll tell him I suddenly felt sick.

STEVE: He won't bat an eye at that excuse, but he'll be thinking something is fishy.

JOAN: Why do you say that?

STEVE: You're such a lousy liar, and he's a cool dude.

Vocabulary Building

Check the glossary for the definitions of these terms:

➤ to not bat an eye (v.)

➤ to duck (v.)

➤ fishy (adj.)

➤ lousy (adj.)

➤ to outfox (v.)

Write a synonym or synonymous phrase for each term in your notebook.

Other Expressions

to be born yesterday   *to be inexperienced or naive*

close call   *narrow escape*

a cool dude   *a very clever, controlled person*

to cut a class   *to be absent from a class*

Questions

1. Why did Joan duck the teacher?
2. Do you think Joan had a good reason for cutting class?
3. What does Steve think about the teacher?
4. What will Joan say if the teacher asks why she missed class?
5. Does Steve think the teacher will believe Joan? Why or why not?
6. What would you do if you were Joan?

Role Play

In groups of two, role-play the following situation.

Characters:

JOAN   HER TEACHER

Situation:

Joan bumps into her teacher, who wants to know why Joan missed class. Joan gives an excuse, but the teacher is very clever and doesn't accept the excuse readily. Joan keeps trying to talk herself out of trouble.

Discussion Topics

Cutting Class: What are good and what are poor reasons for cutting a class? At many universities and colleges, students are not required to attend classes. What are your views on this policy? Do you think schools should have rules about attendance and lateness? If so, create a list of rules you believe would be fair and reasonable. If not, give your reasons. In your opinion, how should teachers react when students cut class?

School Rules and Regulations: Some colleges have rules against certain forms of dress, smoking, drinking, dancing, holding hands, kissing, radio playing, etc. What rules do you believe a school should have? Why?

Learning English

MARIO: English is driving me crazy!

CHRIS: What's wrong?

MARIO: I thought I knew the meaning of "foxy."

CHRIS: Oh, yes. We talked about it yesterday in class.

MARIO: I don't understand it anymore. I got in Dutch with my girlfriend when I said our secretary was foxy.

CHRIS: You must be kidding! She *is* foxy.

MARIO: Yes, but which one — clever or good-looking?

CHRIS: Actually, both.

Vocabulary Building

Check the glossary for the definitions of these terms:

➤ to be kidding (v.)

➤ foxy (adj.)

Write a synonym or synonymous phrase for each term in your notebook.

Other Expressions

to drive someone crazy   *to annoy or disturb someone*

in Dutch   *in trouble*

Questions

1. Why is English driving Mario crazy?

2. How did Mario get in Dutch with his girlfriend?

3. How could Mario have avoided this problem?

4. Why do you think Mario's girlfriend got angry? Do you think her reaction was justified?

5. What does Chris think about the secretary?

Role Play

In groups of two, role-play the following situation.

Characters:

BILL   LOUISE

Situation:

Bill and Louise have been dating for a few weeks. One day Bill sees Louise having lunch with a man from her office. That evening, Bill gets very angry with Louise because he feels jealous. At first Louise thinks Bill is kidding. When she realizes how jealous he is, she tries to explain the situation.

Discussion Topics

Dealing with Jealousy: Have you ever been jealous? If so, why? What happened? How do you handle a person who becomes jealous?

Finding the Correct Meaning: Many English words have more than one meaning. When you read or hear one of these words, how can you tell which meaning is intended? When you say or write one of these words, how can you make sure other people know which meaning you intend?

Experiential Psychology

Ann: Why are you taking Experiential Psychology?

Betty: I'm not entirely happy with myself. I thought I might get some answers.

Ann: Hmmm, don't you think burrowing into a painful past could make you feel even more unhappy?

Betty: True. But as they say: nothing ventured, nothing gained.

Ann: Why open up a can of worms?

Betty: Hold on a minute! Don't cry wolf. I get college credit for this course, you know.

Ann: I know, but I've steered clear of it. I just can't stand telling strangers about my inner feelings or my personal background.

Betty: That doesn't bother me. We were always open about things like that in my family.

Ann: Not in mine. And seeing a shrink was definitely considered shameful.

Betty: Really? Actually, I might become a psychologist.

Ann: Well, I'll never come to see you! I prefer to let sleeping dogs lie.

Vocabulary Building

Check the glossary for the definitions of these terms:

➤ to cry wolf (v.)

➤ Let sleeping dogs lie. (p/s)

➤ to open (up) a can of worms (v.)

➤ to steer clear of (v.)

Write a synonym or synonymous phrase for each term in your notebook.

Other Expressions

to burrow   *to dig into*

can't stand   *can't tolerate*

Hold on a minute! *Wait! Be patient!*

Nothing ventured, nothing gained. *If you don't try to do something, you will never achieve it or profit from it.*

open *straightforward; honest*

shrink *a psychoanalyst or psychotherapist*

Questions

1. Why is Betty taking Experiential Psychology?
2. Why doesn't Ann want to take the course?
3. Why does Betty tell Ann not to "cry wolf"?
4. Was Betty's family open about their inner feelings?
5. How did Ann's family feel about seeing a "shrink"?
6. What does Betty plan to do?

Role Play

In groups of two, role-play the following situation.

Characters:

MARIO   A PSYCHIATRIST

Situation:

Mario has not been able to sleep at night since his brother died in a car accident. At the suggestion of his psychology teacher, Mario visits a psychiatrist. The first half hour is free, but a whole hour costs seventy dollars. Mario knows that he needs help, but he is worried about paying so much to get it. He discusses his concerns with the psychiatrist.

Discussion Topics

Personal Feelings: What do you consider to be "personal information"? Do you believe it would be beneficial or harmful to reveal your personal background in a psychology class? How do you feel about telling your inner feelings to acquaintances? What topics would you discuss only with a close friend? Are there any taboo subjects, subjects you would discuss with no one?

Seeing a "Shrink": What are the differences between psychology and psychiatry? Would you agree to talk about your personal life with a psychologist or a psychiatrist in private? Why do you think psychotherapy has become so popular among certain groups of people in the United States? On the other hand, why do other people make fun of psychologists and psychiatrists?

Problems with Studying

JOAN: I can't seem to get my act together this semester.

ANDY: Are you having any special problems with studying?

JOAN: The assignments are so long and confusing. It'll take forever to complete them.

ANDY: I've never seen such a hangdog expression! Is there anything I can do to help?

JOAN: I've been floundering around here for hours.

ANDY: Show me one of your assignments. If we can't understand it, we can always break it down into steps.

JOAN: OK, here. Let's see if you can make heads or tails out of this.

ANDY: *(while looking at the assignment sheet)* You're supposed to write about some legal issue. Did you discuss any in class?

JOAN: Well, I remember one day we had a heated discussion about speed limits. It really ticked me off. I mean, one guy thought there shouldn't be any at all!

ANDY: Good. It sounds like you're interested in that topic. Now let's go to the library and find some articles about it.

Vocabulary Building

Check the glossary for the definitions of these terms:

➤ to flounder around (v.)

➤ hangdog (adj.)

Write a synonym or synonymous phrase for each term in your notebook.

Other Expressions

to make heads or tails out of *to understand*

to get one's act together   *to get organized; to be in control*

to tick someone off   *to make someone angry*

Questions

1. What is Joan's problem?
2. In your opinion, why does Andy want to help her?
3. How does Andy try to help Joan?
4. What school subject do you think they are going to work on?
5. What topic is Joan interested in? What ticked her off about it?
6. What could be the title of Joan's paper, based on what you know?
7. Where are Andy and Joan going to get information?

Role Play

In groups of three, role-play the following situation.

Characters:

PETRA   A CLASSMATE   THE PROFESSOR

Situation:

Petra is in an education class on school law. The professor is talking about the Supreme Court decision of Lau vs. Nichols in 1974. Petra can't remember what the case was about. The professor calls on Petra and asks her the importance of this court case. A classmate sitting behind Petra whispers "bilingual education for language minorities." Petra repeats this, and the professor is satisfied with her answer. Next the professor calls on the classmate to elaborate. After class, Petra thanks her classmate for helping out.

Discussion Topics

School Problems: Discuss any problems you have with school. Which problems can be solved easily, and which ones are very difficult? What steps can you take to solve a problem? How many students in the class experience the same problems? Within your time limits, try to give solutions to as many students' problems as possible. Or, choose the most common problem and work out a solution for it together.

Favorite and Least Favorite Subjects: Which subjects do you enjoy studying the most? Why? Which subjects do you dislike? Which are boring to you? Why? Discuss your favorite subject areas and tell what you have gained personally, socially, and professionally from studying one of them.

A Sick Classmate

HELEN: Hi, Maria. How are you?

MARIA: Not so good.

HELEN: It sounds like you have a frog in your throat.

MARIA: I guess so. I have a headache, too.

HELEN: Here, take some cough drops. They're nonprescriptive.

MARIA: Mmmm. That does feel good. Where did you get these?

HELEN: At the drugstore around the corner. Say, how are you going to give your speech to the class?

MARIA: Oh, don't bring it up. I get butterflies in my stomach just thinking about it.

HELEN: You'll be skating on thin ice if you don't do it. There are no makeups.

MARIA: Thanks for making me feel worse.

HELEN: I'm sorry about that. Is there anything I can do to help?

MARIA: I don't think so, but thanks for asking. Sorry for being such a crab.

HELEN: No problem. I understand.

Vocabulary Building

Check the glossary for the definitions of these terms:

➤ crab (n.) ➤ to have a frog in one's throat (v.)

➤ to get butterflies in one's stomach (v.)

Write a synonym or synonymous phrase for each term in your notebook.

Other Expressions

to bring something up *to mention something*

makeup *the opportunity given by a teacher to do an assignment or take a test at a later time*

to skate on thin ice *to be in a risky situation*

Questions

1. How does Maria feel?
2. What does Maria's voice sound like?
3. What does Helen offer Maria?
4. How does Maria feel about giving her speech?
5. How will Maria's sickness be a problem?
6. How does Helen make Maria feel worse?
7. What does Maria apologize for?

Role Play

In groups of three, role-play the following situation.

Characters:

TOM   TOM'S BEST FRIEND   TOM'S NEIGHBOR

Situation:

Tom belongs to his city's International and Cultural Exchange Association. He is going to give the main speech at a program welcoming some visitors from Central and South America. He wants to practice his speech out loud, and he needs some honest criticism and suggestions for improvement. Tom's best friend has offered to be the guinea pig. Since it is summer, an open window allows Tom's friendly but nosy neighbor to hear him, too. The neighbor can't help butting in.

Discussion Topics

Comforting or Taking Care of a Sick Person: How do you comfort an acquaintance who is sick? What do you usually say? What do you do? How would you take care of a friend with a cold or other illness?

Friendship: What does friendship mean to you? How do you cultivate a friendship? How do you keep a friend? What sacrifices are you willing to make for a friend?

On the Telephone: The Mistake

MAT: Hello, Susan?

SUSAN: Yes, this is she. Who is this, please?

MAT: It's Mat. Don't you recognize my voice?

SUSAN: Oh yes, the one in my lit class.

MAT: I was hoping we could study together some evening.

SUSAN: That's a horse laugh. You haven't passed an exam in that class yet.

MAT: Well, if I'd been kowtowing to the teacher the way you have been, I'd be the star student, too.

SUSAN: If you'd been paying attention in class, you wouldn't be calling me to bail you out.

MAT: OK. So I made a mistake. *(after hanging up the phone)* What a shrew!

Vocabulary Building

Check the glossary for the definitions of these terms:

➤ shrew (n.)

➤ That's a horse laugh. (p/s)

Write a synonym or synonymous phrase for each term in your notebook.

Other Expressions

to bail someone out   *to get someone out of trouble*

to kowtow   *to defer to; to fawn over*

lit   *an abbreviation for* literature

the star student   *the best student*

Questions

1. Did Susan recognize Mat's voice?
2. What do you think of Susan's behavior toward Mat?
3. What does Mat accuse Susan of?
4. What kind of student is Mat?
5. What kind of student is Susan?
6. Do you think Mat should have made this telephone call? Why or why not?
7. What does "lit" stand for?

Role Play

In groups of two, role-play the following situation.

Characters:

MAT   A CLASSMATE

Situation:

Mat calls a classmate to ask about studying together and sharing notes taken in class. Mat was absent from one class and needs to find out what he missed. The classmate must decide whether or not to help Mat.

Discussion Topics

A Failing Classmate: Do you think it is your duty to help a failing classmate? If a classmate who was failing called you for help, what would you say or do?

Abbreviations: With a partner, make a list of abbreviations commonly used at school by students and teachers. Present your list to the class, and ask the other students to tell what each abbreviation stands for (for example: lit = literature). Discuss other abbreviations you and your classmates have seen or heard.

On the Telephone: The Favor

JOYCE: Hi, Carl. This is Joyce. How are you?

CARL: Fine, thanks. What's up?

JOYCE: Well, I'm calling from the library on campus. Do you think you could do me a favor?

CARL: What's on your mind?

JOYCE: I was so cocksure of myself that I left my math books at home. Now I need them to study for the test.

CARL: That was a squirrelly thing to do. Where do I come in?

JOYCE: I know what a shark you are in math. I was hoping you could bring your books and help me study.

CARL: Are you trying to pull the wool over my eyes?

JOYCE: No, it's true.

CARL: All right. I need a book at the library anyway. This way I can kill two birds with one stone.

JOYCE: I'd really appreciate it. You're a gem.

Vocabulary Building

Check the glossary for the definitions of these terms:

➤ cocksure (adj.)

➤ to kill two birds with one stone (v.)

➤ shark (n.)

➤ squirrelly (adj.)

Write a synonym or synonymous phrase for each term in your notebook.

Other Expressions

to do someone a favor   *to do something nice for someone*

gem   *a valuable or good person*

on one's mind   *occupying one's thoughts*

to pull the wool over someone's eyes   *to try to fool someone*

What's up?   *What is happening?*

Where do I come in?   *What do you want me to do?*

Questions

1. Why did Joyce call Carl?
2. What did Joyce leave at home?
3. What did Carl think about Joyce's mistake?
4. How did Joyce try to convince Carl to help her?
5. What did he believe she was trying to do?
6. Was Carl polite to Joyce?
7. Why did Carl decide to help Joyce?

Role Play

In groups of four, role-play the following situation.

Characters:

BARRY   A CASHIER   A PHARMACIST   A STORE MANAGER

Situation:

Barry can't find his driver's license. He thinks he left it on the pharmacist's counter at the drugstore when he was there earlier in the day. He had to show it to verify a check he wrote for some medicine. Barry calls the drugstore and reaches the cashier first, next he talks to the pharmacist, and finally he talks to the store manager. Barry explains his problem to every person his call is transferred to.

Discussion Topics

Persuasion: How do you persuade a reluctant person to help you? Think of a favor you want from someone. Then think of ways to persuade the person to do the favor for you. Talk about these methods of persuasion with your classmates.

Killing two birds with one stone: What does it mean to "kill two birds with one stone"? Do you ever try to do this? If so, give some examples. If not, give your reasons. Most Americans are pleased when they can kill two birds with one stone. Is this also true of people from your native country? Why or why not? How do cultural perceptions of time affect the value placed on accomplishing two things with one effort?

The Sociology Class

BETTY: I went to meet you after your class yesterday, but no one was in the room.

BOB: We took a field trip to the city jail.

BETTY: Oh, really? Why?

BOB: It was part of our unit on groups of people who live in confinement. We even saw a bull pen.

BETTY: Weren't you scared?

BOB: I'm no chicken. I look upon such things scientifically.

BETTY: What else did you see?

BOB: One of my classmates interviewed a cat burglar. He lived that way for seven years before he was caught.

BETTY: I guess crime pays.

BOB: Not really.

BETTY: On second thought, he can't live high off the hog where he is.

BOB: Right. And besides, he's in for ten years.

Vocabulary Building

Check the glossary for the definitions of these terms:

➤ bull pen (n.)

➤ cat burglar (n.)

➤ chicken (n.)

➤ to live high off the hog (v.)

Write a synonym or synonymous phrase for each term in your notebook.

Other Expressions

to be in for ten years   *to have ten years to serve in confinement or in prison*
Crime doesn't pay.   *Crime will not benefit a person. (proverb)*
on second thought   *after thinking it over*

Questions

1. Where did the sociology class go?
2. Why did they go there?
3. Whom did one student interview?
4. How did Bob feel about the field trip?
5. What can't the cat burglar do for a while?
6. How long will the cat burglar be in jail?
7. Do Bob and Betty think crime is worthwhile? Why or why not?

Role Play

In groups of two, role-play the following situation.

Characters:

TV REPORTER   CRIMINAL

Situation:

The TV reporter is interviewing a criminal for a special human-interest story on the evening news. (Choose one of the following criminals to portray: a burglar, a spouse murderer, a drunk driver, a corrupt judge, an arsonist, or a rapist.) The TV reporter asks the criminal to explain the reasons for his or her crime and to describe his or her plans for the future.

Discussion Topics

Field Trips: Have you ever gone on a field trip? If so, was it an educational experience? Do you think field trips are a helpful part of the learning process? Why or why not? What kinds of field trips would you like to take?

Crime: Get into small groups and discuss one of these topics:

A.   Is ten years too heavy a punishment for a cat burglar? Why or why not? Do you believe a jail sentence can rehabilitate a criminal? If so, what should the sentence involve for the purpose of rehabilitation?

B.   Consider the problem of overcrowded jails that exists in the United States. One possible solution is to have lawbreakers work outside the jail to pay back the victims of their crime. They must report back to jail once a week. Do you think this is a reasonable solution? Why or why not? What other solutions do you think should be tried? Specify some crimes and the type of punishment you would give for each crime.

Come together as a whole class and let each group report on its topic and solutions.

A Study Session

CHRIS: Hi, Jack. Why don't you come on over to my place tonight?

JACK: Are you having a bull session?

CHRIS: Not really. A bunch of us are going to study for econ together.

JACK: That's a good idea. Where do you live?

CHRIS: Not too far from here. If you meet me at the entrance to this building at seven, I'll give you a ride.

JACK: Great! Let me run a couple of errands first; then I'll be back.

CHRIS: Sure. I'm glad you can make it. Take a gander at the textbook before you come.

JACK:: OK. Oh, and let me have your phone number in case we miss each other.

CHRIS: It's 555-5403. See you later.

JACK: Right. Thanks a lot!

Vocabulary Building

Check the glossary for the definitions of these terms:

➤ bull session (n.)
➤ to take a gander (v.)

Write a synonym or synonymous phrase for each term in your notebook.

Other Expressions

econ   *an abbreviation for* economics

to make it   *to come; to attend something*

to run an errand   *to take a short trip to do a specific thing*

Questions

1. What does Chris invite Jack to do?
2. What subject will the study session be about?
3. Where does Chris live?
4. Where and when will Chris and Jack meet each other?
5. What does Jack need to do before they meet?
6. What will Jack do if they miss each other?
7. How should Jack prepare for the study session?

Role Play

In groups of three, role-play the following situation.

Characters:

JACK   CHRIS   A CALLER

Situation:

Jack returns too late to catch Chris at the building entrance. He goes inside the school building to a public phone. However, someone is using the phone, and this caller doesn't hurry to get off. Jack shows his impatience and the caller finally hangs up; they exchange some words, and then the caller leaves. Jack calls Chris, who gives him directions to his apartment.

Discussion Topics

Study Methods: What are the best ways to study? Is it beneficial for you to study with other people? Why or why not?

Bull Sessions: Do you and your friends ever have bull sessions? If so, what kinds of things do you talk about? Where do you get together? Do you enjoy participating in bull sessions? Why or why not?

The Apology

PAT: What's the matter? You look as if you've lost your best friend.

JOHN: I've really played the goat this time.

PAT: Do you want to tell me about it?

JOHN: Do you see this book?

PAT: It's pretty dog-eared. What happened to it?

JOHN: I dropped it while I was running across the street. A car got to it before I could.

PAT: Is that all? It's not the end of the world, you know.

JOHN: My professor lent it to me, and now I'm too embarrassed to give it back.

PAT: Don't be such a coward. I'm sure she'll understand if you apologize.

JOHN: I hope you're right.

Vocabulary Building

Check the glossary for the definitions of these terms:

➤ coward (n.)

➤ dog-eared (adj.)

➤ to play the goat (v.)

Write a synonym or synonymous phrase for each term in your notebook.

Other Expressions

It's not the end of the world. *It's not all that bad; this one event won't ruin your whole life.*

to look as if one has lost one's best friend *to look very sad and depressed*

Questions

1. How does John look?
2. What happened to the book?
3. How does the book look?
4. Is Pat sympathetic?
5. Why is John embarrassed?
6. What is John's opinion of the professor?
7. What is Pat's opinion of the professor?

Role Play

In groups of three, role-play the following situation.

Characters:

JOHN   THE PROFESSOR   THE PROFESSOR'S SECRETARY

Situation:

John goes to Professor Busby's office to return the book he borrowed. First he sees the secretary. John mentions the accident with the book. Upon seeing the dog-eared book, the secretary says, "Oh no, how could you?" After the secretary accuses John of being careless and thoughtless, John loses his courage. He is about to leave when the professor sees him and tells him to come on in.

Discussion Topics

An Embarrassing Situation: Have you ever been embarrassed? If so, what happened? How did you handle the situation? What would you do if you had the chance to deal with it again?

Teacher-Student Relationships: How do teacher-student relationships differ? Have you had the same kind of relationship with all your teachers? How do cultural differences affect teacher-student relationships? Compare and contrast the ways in which students and teachers interact in different cultures.

Unit **5**

The World of Work

Looking for a Job: Before the Interview

JOYCE: I have another job interview on Monday.

ANN: Try not to be so sheepish this time.

JOYCE: I know what you mean. It's a dog-eat-dog world out there.

ANN: You bet. If you don't put up a good front, someone else will get the job.

JOYCE: I plan to go in like a lion.

ANN: Just don't come out like a lamb.

JOYCE: The world is my oyster.

ANN: Now you have the right attitude. Go for it!

Vocabulary Building

Check the glossary for the definitions of these terms:

➤ dog-eat-dog (adj.)

➤ to go in like a lion but come out like a lamb (v.)

➤ sheepish (adj.)

➤ The world is one's oyster. (p/s)

Write a synonym or synonymous phrase for each term in your notebook.

Other Expressions

to put up a good front   *to show your best characteristics; to act brave and confident*

Go for it!   *Do it! Try your best! Grab the opportunity!*

You bet.   *Yes, I agree.*

Questions

1. What do you think happened at Joyce's last job interview?
2. When is it necessary to be like a lion?
3. What is the world of work like, according to Joyce?
4. What is Ann's advice to Joyce?
5. How can a person "put up a good front"?
6. What does Joyce plan to do?
7. What is Joyce's attitude?

Role Play

In groups of three, role-play the following situation.

Characters:

JOYCE   INTERVIEWER 1 (THE PERSONNEL DIRECTOR)
INTERVIEWER 2 (A COMPANY MANAGER)

Situation:

Joyce has answered an ad for a job she believes she can handle. (Determine the kind of job, the salary, and the location). She has an interview with two representatives of the company. After asking several questions about Joyce's reasons for applying for the job and her experience, one interviewer asks an illegal question about Joyce's personal life. Joyce must decide how to handle this. (**Note:** Questions about an applicant's race, gender, religion or creed, culture or ethnic background, and age are considered "illegal." By law, applicants are not required to answer such discriminatory questions.)

Discussion Topics

A Job Interview: What are the best ways to impress an interviewer when you're looking for a job? What are the worst ways? How should you prepare for a job interview?

Building Self-Confidence: How can you build confidence in yourself? How can you help increase another person's self-confidence? Do you think self-confidence is important? Why or why not?

Looking for a Job: After the Interview

JACK: Hi, Steve. How's the job search going?

STEVE: I have several interviews lined up for this week.

JACK: Great! I had one yesterday, but it didn't go too well.

STEVE: Why not? What happened?

JACK: I had some tough competition. But on top of that, the person ahead of me told the interviewer I was considering another job.

STEVE: Oh, no! You mean he ratted on you?

JACK: Yes, he really loused up my chances.

STEVE: I'm sorry to hear that. Next time you'd better clam up about your plans.

JACK: I guess I learned the hard way.

STEVE: Anyway, good luck on your search.

JACK: Thanks. The same to you.

Vocabulary Building

Check the glossary for the definitions of these terms:

➤ to clam up (v.)   ➤ to rat on (v.)

➤ to louse up (v.)

Write a synonym or synonymous phrase for each term in your notebook.

Other Expressions

to learn something the hard way   *to learn something from an unpleasant experience*

lined up   *planned or arranged*

on top of that   *in addition to that*

Questions

1. What has Steve lined up for this week?
2. How did Jack's job interview go yesterday?
3. How did the other interviewee ruin Jack's chances for the job?
4. Why do you think the other interviewee ratted on Jack?
5. What did Steve suggest?
6. What did Jack learn the hard way?
7. What is an example of a dog-eat-dog world?

Role Play

In groups of four, role-play the following situation.

Characters:

A THREE-PERSON SEARCH COMMITTEE   AN INTERVIEWEE

Situation:

The interviewee is applying for a position that offers a three-year contract, exceptional benefits, tuition-free courses for professional development, four weeks of paid vacation per year, and an annual salary of $28,000. (Determine the type of job and the location.) One of the search committee members explains the position and describes its positive aspects and two possibly negative aspects. Another interviewer asks about the applicant's experience, and the third interviewer asks about the applicant's future plans. In addition to answering the committee's questions, the interviewee explains his or her special credentials and skills.

Discussion Topics

Job Hunting: Discuss "the job of job hunting." What kinds of preparation and materials do you need if you are looking for a full-time, long-term position? What do you need to do to find such a job?

Work Experience: What kinds of paid or volunteer work experience have you had? What did you learn from each job, if anything? What kind of job would you like to have now? Why?

Officemates

CHRIS: George is really getting on my nerves.

PAT: What do you mean?

CHRIS: At the elevator today, he acted as if he had ants in his pants.

PAT: He doesn't have much patience.

CHRIS: Even at his desk he couldn't sit still, and then at lunch he wolfed down his food.

PAT: Oh, I know. He came over to our table and wormed his way into our conversation. He just sat down and started talking away.

CHRIS: He doesn't have good manners, that's for sure!

Vocabulary Building

Check the glossary for the definitions of these terms:

➤ to have ants in one's pants (v.)　　➤ to wolf down (v.)

Write a synonym or synonymous phrase for each term in your notebook.

Another Expression

to get on one's nerves　*to irritate or bother a person*

Questions

1. How does Chris feel about George?

2. What did George do at the elevator?

3. What did George do at lunch?

4. Do you think George is impatient or impolite?

5. How did he behave impatiently (if you think he's impatient)?

6. How did he behave impolitely (if you think he's impolite)?

7. How should George have approached his officemates in the cafeteria?

8. Do you think Chris is overly critical of George? Why or why not?

9. What do you usually do to show impatience?

Role Play

In groups of four, role-play the following situation.

Characters:

"Antsy"   "Cool"   "Scaredy-cat"   "Technician"

Situation:

Four people are stuck in an elevator between the sixteenth and seventeenth floors of a modern high-rise office building. "Antsy," a clever but nervous person, immediately starts hitting the emergency button and yelling. "Cool" tries to calm everyone down, especially "Scaredy-cat," who is about to cry. "Technician" offers all kinds of technical information, some of it very scary.

Discussion Topics

Good Manners and Bad Manners: Give some examples of impolite behavior, other than the examples in the dialogue. Then discuss the correct way to behave in various situations, such as making friends, interacting in the classroom, eating a meal, etc. What are considered good table manners in the United States? What are considered bad table manners? How do you deal with bad-mannered (impolite) people? What experiences have you had with polite and with impolite people?

A Problem with a Bad-Mannered Family Member or Acquaintance: Discuss one of these situations:

A. If George were your brother, how would you handle his bad manners? What would you say? What kind of advice would you give him?

B. If George were your classmate, what would you say to him? Would you ignore his behavior? If he constantly interrupted in class, how would you handle the situation?

The Stock Market

CARL: What line of work is your father in?

SAM: He was in commodities; he's retired now.

CARL: So he played the market, did he?

SAM: Yes, he did. In our home we always knew whether it was a bullish market or a bearish market.

CARL: Was he successful at it?

SAM: Oh yes, for the most part. During the last bullish market, he made a killing and pulled out.

CARL: In that case, since my piggy bank's empty, you can pay for lunch.

SAM: Hold your horses! He invested the money for our future. On the other hand, if I pay for our lunch now, then you're on for next time.

CARL: That seems fair enough.

Vocabulary Building

Check the glossary for the definitions of these terms:

➤ bearish (adj.)

➤ bullish (adj.)

➤ to hold one's horses (v.)

➤ piggy bank (n.)˙

Write a synonym or synonymous phrase for each term in your notebook.

Other Expressions

to be on for   *to be responsible for; to be the one to do something*

to make a killing   *to be successful by making a lot of money*

on the other hand   *from another point of view*

to play the market   *to participate in trading; to invest in stocks and bonds*

to pull out   *to quit*

Questions

1. What line of work was Sam's father in?
2. What kind of market is good for investing?
3. How successful was Sam's father?
4. Is Sam's father still playing the market? Why or why not?
5. Why does Carl think Sam should pay for lunch?
6. What did Sam's father do with the money he made?
7. Who is going to pay for lunch? Under what conditions will he do it?

Role Play

In groups of three, role-play the following situation.

Characters:

SAM   A PATIENT FRIEND   A DISGUSTED FRIEND

Situation:

At dinner with two friends, Sam is bragging about his father's success and his family's rich lifestyle — even though his father recently invested most of his fortune in a company that went bankrupt. The patient friend humors Sam, but the disgusted friend becomes bored and irritated with Sam's constant bragging and makes several sarcastic comments. He also teases Sam about treating them to dinner and other activities.

Discussion Topics

Money: When you were a child, did you save money in a piggy bank? If not, how did you save money? How do you save money now?

Investments: What are your plans for future investments? What do you think is the best way to invest money? How do you (plan to) make money? Is it important to you to make a lot of money? How much money will satisfy you, and why?

In and Around the City

Traffic Jam

MARIA: Hi! How come you came late for work this morning?

STELLA: Heavy traffic and road hogs. There was one guy who thought he owned the road. The rest of the traffic was snail-paced.

MARIA: Maybe you should have left the house earlier. Traffic is part of city life.

STELLA: No doubt about it. If there isn't a road hog, there's always someone who worms his way ahead of you.

MARIA: Just be grateful you didn't get caught in a traffic jam. But don't worry; I covered for you and said you had never been late before.

STELLA: Thanks a lot! I appreciate your help.

MARIA: Any time. I know you would do the same for me.

Vocabulary Building

Check the glossary for the definitions of these terms:

➤ road hog (n.)   ➤ to worm one's way (v.)

➤ snail-paced (adj.)

Write a synonym or synonymous phrase for each term in your notebook.

Other Expressions

to cover for someone   *to protect someone (who might get into trouble) by making an excuse or telling a lie*

how come   *why*

traffic jam   *such heavy traffic that the cars can't move*

Questions

1. Why was Stella late?
2. What should Stella have done?

---

3. What is a traffic jam?
4. How did Maria help Stella?
5. Is Stella late very often?
6. What does Maria mean by saying "I know you would do the same for me"?
7. What do you do when you're in a traffic jam?

Role Play

In groups of three, role-play the following situation.

Characters:

STELLA   GAS STATION ATTENDANT   ROAD HOG

Situation:

Stella stops at a gas station and sees the Cadillac that has been hogging the road. The Caddy owner, a middle-aged and well-dressed person, walks over to Stella and criticizes her for tailgating. Stella must decide how to react. The gas station attendant overhears their conversation and adds his or her own opinion.

Discussion Topics

Driving in the City: How is driving in the city different than driving in a small town or in the country? How are road hogs handled in each situation? What is your definition of a "good driver"?

Showing Anger: When you are angry with another driver, what do you usually say? (Translate the expressions into English.) What kinds of gestures do you use (if any)? Is it acceptable for a man to gesture in certain ways, but not for a woman? What might an angry American do? Share what you know about gestures of contempt or anger in various cultures. In what situations might you use certain gestures? Which gestures are dangerous to use?

Male and Female Drivers: In your opinion, do men drive differently than women do? If so, describe how and tell why. Statistics show that women are generally safer drivers than men. Why do you think this is true? Why do you think young males (ages sixteen to twenty-five) are the most dangerous group of drivers on the road?

Lost and Late

MAT: I'm sorry I'm late. I went on a wild-goose chase trying to get here.

BETTY: Didn't you get the right directions?

MAT: I thought so. I got off the expressway at Ogden, but the main road didn't have a street sign. At this time of the evening it's hard to see, too.

BETTY: You were supposed to take Ohio, not Ogden. No wonder you got lost.

MAT:: In that strange neighborhood I almost lost my nerve, too.

BETTY: I bet you felt like a fish out of water.

MAT: You know it. But an elderly man came by and helped me.

BETTY: You were lucky.

Vocabulary Building

Check the glossary for the definitions of these terms:

➤ a fish out of water (n.)　　　➤ wild-goose chase (n.)

Write a synonym or synonymous phrase for each term in your notebook.

Other Expressions

to lose one's nerve　*to lose confidence; to get scared*

no wonder　*not surprising*

Questions

1. Why was Mat late?
2. Where did he get off the expressway?

3. Where should he have gotten off the expressway?
4. How did Mat feel in the strange neighborhood?
5. How did Mat finally find his way?
6. How did Betty express her sympathy with Mat's situation?

Role Play

In groups of two, role-play the following situation.

Characters:

TERRY   A STRANGER

Situation:

Terry is on his way to visit a sick friend in another town, but he can't find the hospital. It is getting dark and he is having trouble seeing the street signs. He sees a stranger walking down a street, so he pulls over and asks for directions to the hospital. The stranger gives him excellent directions and says a few kind words. Mat is relieved and thankful.

Discussion Topics

A Wild-Goose Chase: How can a person avoid going on a wild-goose chase? What should you do before visiting a place for the first time? What is the best way to give directions? Are you good at giving or following directions? Why or why not?

A Fish Out of Water: Have you ever felt out of place, like a fish out of water? Tell about the incident. Then ask your classmates to offer ways to remedy the feeling. Consider each suggestion and decide which one would have been best for you in the situation you described. Explain why you think it's the best suggestion.

The Sears Tower

ANDY: Look! We've got a bird's-eye view of Chicago from up here.

BARBARA: It's fantastic.

ANDY: I'm glad it's not raining cats and dogs anymore.

BARBARA: You never know what the weather will be like in Chicago.

ANDY: That's true. They say if you don't like the weather today, wait until tomorrow.

BARBARA: Do you see the John Hancock Building over there? Nearby, at Water Tower Place, we can get a hackney coach.

ANDY: We paid for this view, so let's get the most out of it.

BARBARA: Well, we can't stay up here all day. I'm so hungry I could eat a horse.

ANDY: That's funny, coming from someone who eats like a bird.

Vocabulary Building

Check the glossary for the definitions of these terms:

➤ a bird's-eye view (n.)   ➤ I'm so hungry, I could eat a horse. (p/s)

➤ to eat like a bird (v.)   ➤ to rain cats and dogs (v.)

➤ hackney coach (n.)

Write a synonym or synonymous phrase for each term in your notebook.

Other Expressions

to get the most out of something   *to take advantage of something to the fullest*

If you don't like the weather today, wait until tomorrow.   *The weather is very changeable.*

Questions

1. Where are Andy and Barbara?

2. What kind of view do they have?
3. What is the weather like?
4. What do some people say about the weather in Chicago?
5. Why does Barbara want to leave?
6. Why does Andy say Barbara's comment is "funny"?
7. What can you see from the top of the Sears Tower?

Role Play

In groups of four, role-play the following situation.

Characters:

A TOUR AGENT   A TOUR GUIDE   ANDY   BARBARA

Situation:

Andy and Barbara are visiting San Francisco and they want to take a tour of the city. The tour agent explains two different tours, one of which the couple chooses. On the tour, however, they find out that the guide is cutting the tour short by not stopping at some places. At first Andy and Barbara are polite about expressing their disappointment, but soon they become angry about the tour guide's attitude. They threaten to complain to the tour company.

Discussion Topics

A Tour of the City: In groups of four or five, discuss and plan a one-day tour of your city (or a nearby city). Choose the most important places to visit. Give reasons for your choices.

Skyscrapers: What do you think of skyscrapers? Would you like to live or work in one? Why or why not? Have you ever been to the top of a very tall building? If so, where was it? What did you see?

Cities of the World: Which major cities have you toured? What do you remember best about each one? If you haven't toured any, which major cities would you like to visit? Why? What would you like to see and experience in one of the world's great cities?

At the Restaurant

TOM: One thing I like about a big city is the choice of restaurants.

STELLA: I agree. Isn't the atmosphere great here?

TOM: It certainly is. I've been squirrelling away money all winter for this occasion.

STELLA: I'm glad you got the old sheepskin and decided to celebrate with me.

WAITER: May I take your order?

TOM: Just a minute. *(to Stella)* The waiter is starting to hound us, so we'd better place our orders.

STELLA: I'll have the house special.

WAITER: You won't be disappointed. The fish was flown in today.

TOM: It sounds good. I'll have the same. *(to Stella)* Are you having anything to drink?

STELLA: No, let's pass on the cocktails. You have to drive us home, you know.

TOM: That's right. I'll have the yogurt drink, though. It's nonalcoholic.

STELLA: That's a bit too strange for me. I'll stick with ice water.

WAITER: Will there be anything else? We have a special dessert menu.

STELLA: I think I'll decide on that later, please.

TOM: Me, too.

WAITER: Fine. I'll be back with your salads in a minute.

Vocabulary Building

Check the glossary for the definitions of these terms:

➤ cocktail (n.)

➤ to hound (v.)

➤ sheepskin (n.)

➤ to squirrel away (v.)

Write a synonym or synonymous phrase for each term in your notebook.

Other Expressions

to pass on something   *to refuse something*

to stick with   *to have; to remain with*

Questions

1. What kind of restaurant are Tom and Stella at?
2. Why have they come to this restaurant? What is the occasion?
3. What do they order?
4. Why do they decide to pass on the cocktails? What kind of drinks do they order?
5. Why does Stella turn down the yogurt drink?
6. Do you think the waiter is pushy or polite? How can you tell?
7. Are Tom and Stella going to have dessert?

Role Play

In groups of four, role-play the following situation.

Characters:

TWO SIBLINGS, ONE OLDER AND MORE SOPHISTICATED THAN THE OTHER

HOST OR HOSTESS   WAITER OR WAITRESS

Situation:

Two siblings go to a fancy restaurant to celebrate their graduations, one from high school and the other from college. The college graduate is treating the younger sibling. The host or hostess greets them and escorts them to a table next to the kitchen. They refuse this table and are shown to a much better one. The waiter or waitress brings the menus and makes some suggestions. The siblings take a few minutes to look over the menus and then order when the waiter or waitress returns.

Discussion Topics

Celebrating a Graduation: How would you like to celebrate your graduation? Describe the occasion: tell where you would like to be, whom you would like to celebrate with, and whether or not you would like to receive special gifts.

A Special Restaurant: Recommend a special restaurant. Describe the atmosphere, the service, the prices, and the kinds of dishes and drinks that are available.

Drinking Alcoholic Beverages: What do you think about drinking? What are its harmful effects? If you were/are a parent, would/do you drink alcoholic beverages in front of your children? Why or why not? In your opinion, what kinds of laws should there be about drunk driving? What are the best ways to prevent people from drinking and driving?

Public Transportation

HENRY: Excuse me for bothering you. Is this the right platform for going south?

OLD MAN: Yes, it is. Where are you going?

HENRY: Downtown.

OLD MAN: You're on the right platform all right. You can get on any train that stops here.

HENRY: Thanks a lot. Oh no, it's starting to rain.

OLD MAN: Here's the train. Make like a rabbit and hop to it.

HENRY: *(on the train)* Am I happy the train came when it did. It's pouring cats and dogs out there now.

OLD MAN: How dumb can you get!

HENRY: I beg your pardon?

OLD MAN: I was bats to forget my umbrella today.

HENRY: I forgot mine, too. And I'm going to have to eat crow when I get home.

OLD MAN: Why's that?

HENRY: My mother told me to take an umbrella this morning.

OLD MAN: Well, you can't win them all.

Vocabulary Building

Check the glossary for the definitions of these terms:

➤ bats (adj.)

➤ to eat crow (v.)

➤ to make like a rabbit (v.)

➤ to pour (rain) cats and dogs (v.)

Write a synonym or synonymous phrase for each term in your notebook.

Other Expressions

to hop to it   *to move quickly in a certain direction*

How dumb can you get! *someone (either the speaker, the listener, or a third person) has done something very dumb*

I beg your pardon? *Excuse me. (used with rising intonation if the listener is confused)*

You can't win them all. *It's not possible to win at everything you do. You can't always be right.*

Questions

1. Where is Henry?
2. Which direction does Henry want to go? What is his destination?
3. Which train does Henry need to take?
4. Why does the old man tell Henry "to hop to it"?
5. What is the weather like?
6. What has the old man forgotten?
7. Why will Henry have to eat crow when he gets home?
8. What does the old man mean by his last comment?

Role Play

In groups of two, role-play the following situation.

Characters:

HENRY   HENRY'S MOTHER

Situation:

Henry arrives home soaking wet. He got caught in the rain when he got off the train on his way home. His mother opens the door and sees Henry looking like a drowned rat. She remembers that she told Henry to take an umbrella that morning and teases him for forgetting it.

Discussion Topics

Using Public Transportation: Tell about your means of transportation to and from school or work. Is it usually on time? Is it safe? Is it comfortable? How long does it take you to travel back and forth?

Comparing Methods of Transportation: Describe another method of transportation you have used. Compare it to the one you described above. How are they similar? How are they different?

The City Animal

JOSIE: I was brought up on a farm, but I think I'm becoming a city animal.

CHRIS: Oh, why's that?

JOSIE: My cousin came to visit and was shocked at how I've changed.

CHRIS: Let's have a rundown on what you mean.

JOSIE: He was scared as a rabbit when I jaywalked.

CHRIS: So you've learned the art of dodging cars, have you?

JOSIE: Not only that, I told him I'd rather take him to the theater than spend time in the kitchen.

CHRIS: He was expecting an elaborate, home-cooked meal, I suppose. Did you go to a good play?

JOSIE: Unfortunately, it was a turkey. You should have heard the catcalls. But we went to an outdoor concert which was great.

CHRIS: Has your cousin gotten used to city life yet, or does he think it's for the birds?

JOSIE: I believe he's taking to it like a duck to water.

Vocabulary Building

Check the glossary for the definitions of these terms:

➤ catcall (n.)

➤ city animal (n.)

➤ for the birds (adj.)

➤ to jaywalk (v.)

➤ like a duck to water (adv.)

➤ scared as a rabbit (adj.)

➤ turkey (n.)

Write a synonym or synonymous phrase for each term in your notebook.

Another Expression

rundown   *an item-by-item report; a summary*

Questions

1. Where was Josie brought up?

2. What has Josie become?

3. Where did Josie take her cousin?

4. What scared Josie's cousin?

5. How was the play?

6. What did the audience do?

7. What does Josie's cousin think about city life now?

Role Play

In groups of four, role-play the following situation.

Characters:

TWO CITY ANIMALS   TWO COUNTRY DWELLERS

Situation:

Four high-school friends meet for the first time in ten years at a class reunion. They decide they would like to spend a day together with their families. However, they can't decide where to meet. Two of the friends live out in the country, while the other two live in a big city. The country dwellers tell about the benefits and beauty of their area, but the city animals describe the excitement, variety, and culture of the city.

Discussion Topics

Changes: How have you changed since you came here to live? What are some reasons for the changes in you? Do you think your changes are good, bad, or just necessary?

Visitors: Have you had visitors from your former hometown? If so, where did you take them? What was their reaction to your life here? Have you ever visited a place you used to live? If so, what changes did you find?

Cultural Differences and Reactions

Introductions and Nicknames

CARL: Barbara, I'd like you to meet my friend. This is Tanya. *(looking at Tanya)* Barbara is our hostess.

BARBARA: I'm so glad you could make it tonight. Please call me Barb.

TANYA: I'm sorry. I didn't get your name. My English isn't very good.

BARBARA: *(more slowly)* Barbara. But everyone calls me Barb for short.

CARL: Barb is her nickname. We often use nicknames to be friendly.

BARBARA: You know, Tanya, I've been badgering Carl to meet you. I hope you'll like living in the United States.

TANYA: Thank you for inviting me. Everyone is so friendly here.

BARBARA: It's nice of you to say that. Please tell me something about your native country.

CARL: Just let me introduce her around first. We'll be back in two shakes of a lamb's tail.

TANYA: Nice meeting you, Barb.

BARBARA: Nice meeting you, Tanya, and I think your English is terrific.

Vocabulary Building

Check the glossary for the definitions of these terms:

➤ to badger (v.)   ➤ in two shakes of a lamb's tail (adv.)

Write a synonym or synonymous phrase for each term in your notebook.

Other Expressions

to introduce someone around *to introduce someone to several other people, especially at a party or a group meeting*

to make it *to come; to attend something*

Questions

1. Whom did Carl introduce around?
2. Who is Tanya? Where do you think she is from?
3. What is Barbara's nickname?
4. What has Barbara been doing in order to meet Tanya?
5. What does Barbara want to know about Tanya?
6. Why doesn't Carl let Barb talk to Tanya some more?
7. How soon will Carl return Tanya to Barb?
8. Why does Barb compliment Tanya about her English?

Role Play

In groups of five, role-play the following situation.

Characters:

ANN   BOB   TOM   TONY   LIZ

Situation:

Bob is taking his roommate Tom to Ann's holiday open house. Tom is from a foreign country, so Bob wants to help him make friends in the United States. When they arrive at the open house, Ann greets them. Then Bob introduces Tom to Tony and Liz, two other guests. Ann invites them to help themselves to the holiday food spread out on a long, decorated table. This holiday is new to Tom, so the other guests answer his questions about the food, decorations, and other holiday customs.

Discussion Topics

Nicknames: What do you think of the American custom of giving people nicknames? Do you have a nickname? If so, what is it? If not, what kind of nickname would you like to have (if any)?

Introductions: In what situation would you introduce a friend to other people or to another person? How would you do it according to the customs of your culture? Discuss cultural differences in introductions, such as who is introduced first, who can make the introductions, and where and when they may be made.

Formality vs. Informality: Americans are known for their casual dress, manners, and attitudes. Describe some specific ways in which Americans are informal. Which ways do you find strange or offensive? Which do you like? Why?

Being a Foreigner

FOREIGNER: I don't think I can take any more of this culture.

AMERICAN: Hold your horses! You have a lot going for you.

FOREIGNER: I feel like going back home.

AMERICAN: Maybe you need a vacation from English.

FOREIGNER: You know it. If I'd had any horse sense, I wouldn't have come here in the first place.

AMERICAN: It hasn't been a complete loss. Look at all the English you've learned already!

FOREIGNER: Do you really think so?

AMERICAN: I certainly do.

FOREIGNER: I guess I can stick it out a while longer. Still, it's like holding an eel by the tail.

AMERICAN: If it gets too bad, you can always change your mind.

FOREIGNER: I'm not too sure I can change horses in midstream. I guess I'll just have to put up with it.

Vocabulary Building

Check the glossary for the definitions of these terms:

➤ to change (swap) horses in midstream (v.)

➤ to hold an eel by the tail (v.)

➤ to hold one's horses (v.)

➤ horse sense (n.)

Write a synonym or synonymous phrase for each term in your notebook.

Other Expressions

to change one's mind   *to change one's opinion or decision* to have a lot going for one   *to have many advantages*

to put up with   *to tolerate*

to stick something out   *to endure something*

to take something   *to tolerate or endure something*

Questions

1. What is the foreigner's problem?
2. What does he or she want to do?
3. How does the American react?
4. What does the American suggest?
5. Why does the foreigner think he or she doesn't have any horse sense?
6. How does the foreigner feel?
7. Is it true that "you can always change your mind"? Why or why not?

Role Play

In groups of two, role-play the following situation.

Characters:

A FOREIGNER   AN AMERICAN

Situation:

The foreigner and the American are discussing the foreigner's lifestyle in his or her native country. The American asks questions and tries to understand the lifestyle being described. Both friends compare and contrast that life to their life in the United States.

Discussion Topics

Giving Advice: What advice would you give to a friend or relative who is thinking about moving to the United States? Based on your own experiences, do you think he or she should come? If not, give reasons for your decision. If so, tell what plans the person should make before coming, and what he or she should do upon arrival.

Moving to the United States: Are you or your parents or other relatives sorry you came here? Why or why not? What might you have done if you hadn't come here? Is it possible for you to return to your home country? Why or why not?

Coping with a Different Culture: Explain your experiences with living in a different culture. How have you been treated? What has been difficult for you? What has been fairly easy? What strategies have worked for you in coping with cultural differences? What specific actions have you taken?

Women's Tears

MAN: One thing that gets my goat about women is their tears.

WOMAN: That's because men always shrink from emotions. Crying is good for a person.

MAN: It doesn't accomplish anything. Mostly it's used as a red herring, to avoid the real problem.

WOMAN: I don't think you're being fair.

MAN: You women are good at shedding crocodile tears.

WOMAN: No, tears are a release from frustration or grief. They make you feel better afterwards. Crying usually helps me to see my problems more clearly.

MAN: Not me. It makes me feel like a rat.

Vocabulary Building

Check the glossary for the definitions of these terms:

➤ crocodile tears (n.)

➤ to get one's goat (v.)

➤ rat (n.)

➤ red herring (n.)

Write a synonym or synonymous phrase for each term in your notebook.

Questions

1. What is the man's complaint about women?

2. According to the man, why do women cry?

3. What is the woman's opinion about crying?

4. How do tears make the man feel?

5. Do you agree with the man or the woman? Why?

6. In your opinion, what are some situations that deserve "a good cry"?

Role Play

In groups of three, role-play the following situation.

Characters:

MR. CARP   MRS. CARP   A NEIGHBOR

Situation:

Mr. Carp is watching a baseball game on TV one Sunday afternoon while his wife tries to put the place in order. As she removes some piles of paper and dusts, Mr. Carp makes sarcastic comments about her. She becomes defensive and replies with sarcasm as well, accusing him of being a couch potato, for example. A friendly neighbor living in the apartment next door overhears them and yells, "Life is too short to fight! Lighten up!" Then Mr. and Mrs. Carp direct their attention to the neighbor.

Discussion Topics

Cultural Differences in Men's and Women's Behavior: Do you think crying is equally appropriate for men and women? In your culture, what kinds of behavior are appropriate for men but not for women and vice versa?

Someone's Crying: Does crying ever help you feel better? What are the benefits of crying, if any? What do you do when someone you know starts crying? Are there culturally appropriate ways to deal with someone who is crying? Should your response depend on the situation? If so, give specific examples.

The North and the South

BARRY: Hi, Pat. Where have you been all week?

PAT: I went to visit a cousin in Georgia.

BARRY: What did you think of the South?

PAT: Understanding the dialect was a bear at first, but my cousin translated for me.

BARRY: Did you notice any differences in behavior compared to the North?

PAT: Oh, yes. Everyone acted like a dog with two tails, and people usually said "you all" when talking to more than one person.

BARRY: I spent some time in Texas once. It was the first time I ever ate hush puppies.

PAT: I've tried those. I liked Georgia so much that I'm thinking of moving there.

BARRY: I don't think you should change horses in midstream.

PAT: I could finish out the year here and then leave.

BARRY: Excuse me for fawning, but I'll miss you if you go.

Vocabulary Building

Check the glossary for the definitions of these terms:

➤ bear (n.)

➤ to change (swap) horses in midstream (v.)

➤ a dog with two tails (n.)

➤ to fawn (v.)

➤ hush puppies (n.)

Write a synonym or synonymous phrase for each term in your notebook.

Questions

1. Where was Pat?

2. What cultural differences did Pat notice?

3. What did Pat's cousin have to do for Pat?

4. Where did Barry eat hush puppies for the first time?

5. According to Pat, how do people act and talk in the South?

6. What are Pat's plans for the future?

7. How does Barry feel about Pat's plans?

8. What does Barry wish?

Role Play

In groups of two, role-play the following situation.

Characters:

AMY   CHRIS

Situation:

Amy arrives to tell Chris that she is leaving to take a job opportunity in another state. This is bad news for Chris, who points out the importance of their close friendship and the advantages of staying. Amy has to explain her decision and comfort Chris.

Discussion Topics

Cultural Differences in the United States: Tell where you have been in the United States, and describe some differences between various parts of the country. Why do you think these differences exist? Which ethnic groups live in your city or region? Where do they live? What are their cultural differences? Do the members of one ethnic group prefer to live in the same neighborhood or section of the city? Is there any discrimination against certain groups in your area? Why or why not?

Cultural Differences in Your Native Country: How many languages or dialects are spoken in your native country? What are the different ethnic groups in the country? Where do the members of each group live? Are there differences between the people who live in the southern part and those who live in the northern part of your country? Are any particular groups discriminated against? If so, who are they, and what are the reasons for the discrimination?

American Food

JACK: Good food at a low price is as scarce as hen's teeth in this country.

MARIO: You can't know a hawk from a handsaw to say that.

JACK: Don't tell me hot dogs and hamburgers are your idea of good food!

MARIO: What about tacos, pizza, buffalo wings, southern fried chicken, and hush puppies?

JACK: All right, you've got me there. But I prefer health food, and for that you have to pay through the nose.

MARIO: That's a horse of a different color. But still, it's not as bad as all that. I know a place where the food is good for your health and your pocketbook. It's called the Heartland.

JACK: I've never heard of it. Let's go there for lunch tomorrow.

MARIO: Great! You'll be in for a big surprise.

Vocabulary Building

Check the glossary for the definitions of these terms:

- as scarce as hen's teeth (adv.)
- buffalo wings (n.)
- a horse of a different color (n.)
- hot dog (n.)
- hush puppies (n.)
- to know a hawk from a handsaw (v.)

Write a synonym or synonymous phrase for each term in your notebook.

Other Expressions

to be in for a surprise *to be due for a surprise*

to change one's mind *to change one's opinion or decision*

health food *food that is believed to promote good health*

to pay through the nose *to pay too much*

You've got me there. *I admit you're right about that.*

Questions

1. What is Jack's opinion of American food?

2. Does Mario agree with Jack? How do you know?

3. What kind of food does Jack prefer?

4. What is "health food"?

5. According to Mario, where can a person eat health food at reasonable prices?

6. What have Mario and Jack agreed to do together?

Role Play

In groups of two, role-play the following situation.

Characters:

Ms. Paten   Minnie Paten, her teenage daughter

Situation:

Ms. Paten and her teenage daughter Minnie are talking about food. Minnie loves junk food, especially candy and chips of all kinds. Ms. Paten tells her daughter about the consequences of such bad eating habits. Minnie is as stubborn as a mule at first, but gradually she begins to listen to her mother's good advice.

Discussion Topics

American Food: What is American food? Are there any kinds of dishes that have been developed in the United States? What kinds of foods have been brought to the United States from other countries? Which "ethnic foods" are the most popular in the United States?

Food Preferences: What is your idea of "good food"? Is it good for you? What is your favorite kind of food?

Health Food: What is nutritious food? What kinds of dishes do you consider truly nutritious? What kinds of dishes are not nutritious, and why?

The Potluck

PAT: Did you have a good time last weekend?

CARL: Yes, I did. I went to a potluck.

PAT: What did you take?

CARL: I took an appetizer, so I had to be on time.

PAT: What kinds of food did they have?

CARL: There were all kinds of international dishes on a long table.

PAT: I hope you didn't make a pig of yourself.

CARL: So do I. But if I did, I wasn't the only one who pigged out.

Vocabulary Building

Check the glossary for the definitions of these terms:

➤ to make a pig of oneself (v.)

➤ to pig out (v.)

Write a synonym or synonymous phrase for each term in your notebook.

Another Expression

potluck   *a party (usually a dinner) to which each guest brings something to eat or drink*

Questions

1. What did Carl do last weekend?

2. What did Carl take?

3. What is a potluck? Use your own words to describe it.

4. What kinds of food were served at the potluck?

5. Did everyone eat a lot at the potluck?

6. Do you have potlucks or similar festivities in your native country? If so, what is the occasion for such an event?

Role Play

In groups of three, role-play the following situation.

Characters:

JOYCE   SUE   SANDY (THE HOST)

Situation:

Joyce and Sue are attending a potluck at the home of their friend Sandy. As they enter the house and are greeted by their friend, they notice that the other guests are arriving with neatly wrapped packages of prepared food. Sandy is responding to each offering with enthusiasm and appreciation. Joyce and Sue feel embarrassed that they did not understand what a potluck meant and arrived empty-handed.

Discussion Topics

A Feast: For what occasions does your family have a big meal? How do you prepare for a feast? What kinds of food and drinks do you usually serve? Who does the cooking? Who does the serving? How is the food served? Is all the food placed on one big table? What kind of food is served first? What kind comes last? Who cleans up afterwards?

Table Manners: Take turns describing the proper ways to serve food and to eat in your culture. If possible, explain reasons for your customs.

Unit 8

Recreation, Vacation, and Sports

Staying on the Team

CAROL: Why are you limping?

BOB: In football practice today, I got a charley horse.

CAROL: Have you done anything for it?

BOB: No, not yet. I just hope the coach still lets me play in the game on Saturday.

CAROL: I'm sure he will. You're too good to give up on, and I've got that straight from the horse's mouth.

BOB: Really? What did the coach say about me?

CAROL: He said you were a real tiger. So just take a hot bath and rub some liniment on your leg.

BOB: That sounds like a good idea.

Vocabulary Building

Check the glossary for the definitions of these terms:

➤ charley horse (n.)

➤ straight from the horse's mouth (adv.)

➤ tiger (n.)

Write a synonym or synonymous phrase for each term in your notebook.

Another Expression

to give up on someone   *to forget about or abandon someone*

Questions

1. Why is Bob limping?
2. What is Bob afraid of?

3. How does Carol know that Bob won't lose his position on the team?

4. What does Carol suggest?

5. What did the coach say about Bob?

Role Play

In groups of three, role-play the following situation.

Characters:

SWIM COACH   TWO MEMBERS OF THE SWIM TEAM

Situation:

After a swimming meet, the coach talks to the swimmers. The coach is very disappointed because the swim meet did not go well. First she criticizes the team's poor performance, and then she gives the swimmers a pep talk to encourage them to do better next time. One of the swimmers agrees with everything the coach says, but another swimmer feels the coach is being unfair and keeps making excuses for the team.

Discussion Topics

Sports: What is your opinion about the role of sports in colleges and high schools? Do you think sports scholarships should be awarded? If so, under what circumstances? What kinds of sports should schools encourage? Give reasons for each sport you name. Do you think sports are given too much importance in schools in the United States? Why or why not?

Remedies for Injuries: How should you take care of a charley horse? What are some remedies or treatments for easing sore muscles, aches, and pains?

Soccer vs. Baseball

STELLA: Soccer is much more exciting than baseball.

JOE: I'm not so sure about that.

STELLA: What bugs me about baseball is the way the players just stand around.

JOE: Have you ever seen a batter hit a home run? There's a lot of excitement then.

STELLA: When I see one, I'm buffaloed. Why does the runner slide on the ground?

JOE: He has to touch the base before a player from the other team touches him with the ball in his hand.

STELLA: That doesn't make much sense.

JOE: If you're not going to be pigheaded about it, I'd be glad to teach you about baseball.

STELLA: Thanks. That would make a whale of a difference.

Vocabulary Building

Check the glossary for the definitions of these terms:

➤ buffaloed (adj.)

➤ to bug (v.)

➤ pigheaded (adj.)

➤ a whale of a difference (n.)

Write a synonym or synonymous phrase for each term in your notebook.

Another Expression

to make sense   *to be understandable*

Questions

1. What does Stella think about baseball?
2. What is Joe's reaction to Stella's opinion of baseball?
3. What suggestion does Joe make?
4. What answer does he get?
5. What happens when a batter hits a home run?
6. Why do runners sometimes slide on the ground?

Role Play

In groups of two, role-play the following situation.

Characters:

YOHEI   MICHAEL

Situation:

Yohei is explaining his favorite sport to Michael, who knows little or nothing about the sport. Therefore, Yohei must explain very clearly what kind of sport it is: winter, summer, outdoor, indoor, team, partner, individual, etc. He also must describe any equipment used to play the sport. Michael's comments and questions help Yohei, so that his explanation is neither too simple (and insulting to Michael's intelligence) nor too complicated.

Discussion Topics

Baseball vs. Soccer: Compare the sports of baseball and soccer. Which one is more exciting for you? Why? Should either one be encouraged more than the other in the United States? Give reasons for your answers.

Preferred Sports: Which sport do you prefer to play? Why? How does your favorite sport benefit you? What do you get out of it? Which sport do you prefer to watch? Why?

Camping

JOE: Have you ever gone camping?

ANN: Once. It was really a fishing trip.

JOE: How was it?

ANN: We slept in a pup tent. Every day we caught about a dozen fish.

JOE: Did you eat them all up?

ANN: Of course. I butterflied each one, cleaned it, and fried it over an open fire.

JOE: It sounds as if you had a good time.

ANN: Oh yes, we even played ducks and drakes at a nearby lake. The loser had to clean up after our meals.

JOE: I'm going camping this weekend with a group of friends.

ANN: Be prepared, and have a good time!

Vocabulary Building

Check the glossary for the definitions of these terms:

➤ to butterfly (v.)

➤ ducks and drakes (n.)

➤ pup tent (n.)

Write a synonym or synonymous phrase for each term in your notebook.

Questions

1. What kind of trip did Ann take?
2. What did Ann do with the fish?
3. Where did Ann sleep?

4. What game did Ann's group play?

5. What is Joe going to do this weekend?

6. What kinds of preparations are necessary for a camping trip?

Role Play

In groups of four, role-play the following situation.

Characters:

FOUR FRIENDS

Situation:

Four friends are camping in the wilderness. The weather has turned cold and rainy. Two of the friends want to give up and leave. The other two believe they must show their ability to survive, regardless of the weather. The friends are talking in front of a camp fire they have managed to shield from the pouring rain. Two of the campers talk about their misery, while the other two talk about the importance of endurance and courage.

Discussion Topics

Camping: Have you ever gone camping? If so, where did you go? What activities did you perform? What kinds of food did you prepare? Where did you sleep? Did you enjoy yourself? What would you do differently if you went camping again? If you've never gone camping, would you like to do so? Why or why not? What are some safety rules for camping? Discuss the pros and cons of camping.

Fishing: Have you ever gone fishing? If so, how many fish did you catch? What did you do with the fish? What was the most enjoyable part of fishing? What was the least enjoyable?

Outdoor Games: Describe your favorite outdoor game. How many people does it involve? What kinds of equipment do you need? Where and how often do you play the game?

The Picnic

TOM: What a beautiful day for a picnic!

JANE: With all the food we brought along, we can spend the whole day here.

TOM: Let's get out the barbecue and roast the hot dogs.

JANE: Not yet. It's too early.

TOM: Let me know when you're ready. I'll set it up and prepare the greatest outdoor meal.

JANE: What an eager beaver! I'd rather make a beeline for the beach.

TOM: OK, but no horseplay! Remember, I'm afraid of water.

JANE: I'll treat you with kid gloves.

TOM: That's a comfort.

Vocabulary Building

Check the glossary for the definitions of these terms:

➤ eager beaver (n.)

➤ horseplay (n.)

➤ hot dog (n.)

➤ to make a beeline for (v.)

➤ to treat someone with kid gloves (v.)

Write a synonym or synonymous phrase for each term in your notebook.

Questions

1. What kind of day is it?

2. What does Tom want to do right away?

3. What would Jane like to do instead?

4. How does Tom show that he is an eager beaver?

5. What are Tom and Jane going to do first?

6. What is Tom afraid of?

7. How will Jane help him?

Role Play

In groups of two, role-play the following situation.

Characters:

MICHELLE   GREG

Situation:

Michelle and Greg are planning a picnic. They are discussing where and when they will go, how to get there, and what to take with them. They also must decide who will bring each item. Finally, they talk about what they will do for recreation.

Discussion Topics

Fears: Are you afraid of water? Why or why not? What is your greatest fear? How would you like others to help you with your fear? How would you treat a person who is afraid of water, heights, animals, or anything else that doesn't frighten you?

Picnics: Where do you like to go on picnics? What kinds of foods do you take on a picnic? Do you enjoy barbecuing? Why or why not? How often do you go on picnics? What kind of weather do you think is good for a picnic? What do you do besides eating when you have a picnic?

Back from Vacation

ANN: How was your vacation?

JACK: OK, I guess.

ANN: Didn't you have a good time?

JACK: Yes and no. We stayed in a fleabag, the Royal Palace Hotel.

ANN: It sounds pretty fancy. What went wrong?

JACK: I thought it would be duck soup to just find a place along the road.

ANN: Didn't you make a reservation?

JACK: No, that was the trouble. We had to try a couple of places before we found a vacancy.

ANN: It looks like you were caught in a bind. How long did you have to stay there?

JACK: We had to spend a couple of days because our car broke down. I was ready to cry out "My kingdom for a horse!"

ANN: I hope you found a good grease monkey at least.

JACK: We did, but it took two days for the right part to come in.

ANN: What did you do in the meantime?

JACK: We rented bicycles and rode along a beautiful lake.

ANN: I'm happy to hear that something turned out right.

JACK: Yes. We played cards too, and I won the kitty in a poker game. I blew it all at a French restaurant the next day.

ANN: Easy come, easy go. Now you can rest up by going back to your studies and becoming a bookworm.

JACK: Come to think of it, I'm glad I went on a vacation.

Vocabulary Building

Check the glossary for the definitions of these terms:

➤ bookworm (n.)

➤ duck soup (n.)

➤ fleabag (n.)

➤ grease monkey (n.)

➤ kitty (n.)

➤ My kingdom for a horse! (p/s)

Write a synonym or synonymous phrase for each term in your notebook.

Other Expressions

to be caught in a bind   *to be in a difficult situation*

to blow an amount of money   *to spend or waste that amount of money*

come to think of it   *on second thought; when I reflect on it*

Easy come, easy go.   *When you get something easily, you may lose it just as easily.*

to turn out right   *to end satisfactorily*

Questions

1. Where did Jack stay on his vacation?

2. What went wrong with the vacation?

3. What turned out right?

4. How did Jack win money?

5. What did he do with his winnings?

6. What did Ann mean when she told Jack he could "rest up by going back to his studies and becoming a bookworm"?

7. How did Jack feel about Ann's last comment?

Role Play

In groups of four, role-play the following situation.

Characters:

MR. HOOK   MRS. HOOK   TOM HOOK   TINA HOOK

Situation:

Mr. and Mrs. Hook are taking a long car trip with their children (Tom and Tina) and the family dog. They are going to attend the wedding of a relative. Mr. and Mrs. Hook take turns driving. They have been on the road for two days, and they have about three hundred miles to go. One by one the Hooks become more irritable: the children whine, the dog barks, and the adults try not to lose their patience.

Discussion Topics

Preparing for a Vacation: How should you prepare for a vacation by car in the United States? Share your experiences if you have taken such a trip already. Otherwise, plan a car trip for the future. Tell where you'd like to go and what you'd like to see and do.

The Dream Vacation: What is your idea of a dream vacation? If you had no money or time restrictions, where would you go and what would you do? Why would you enjoy this vacation?

Favorite Vacation: Describe the best vacation you have ever taken. Where did you go? With whom did you travel? What did you see and do? What made the vacation so successful?

Unit 9
The Media

Privacy

BARRY: Did you watch the news on TV last night?

PAT: Yes. I feel terrible about the boy who was kidnapped.

BARRY: Me, too. But what really bugs me is the way the reporters hound people for a story — right in the middle of a crisis.

PAT: A reporter's job is to ferret out the news. But you're right. The media should show more respect for people's privacy.

BARRY: That boy's family sure didn't get any privacy last night! His poor mother was crying while those vultures kept trying to interview her.

PAT: And the poor little boy! He's probably scared as a rabbit. I hope the police can solve this case quickly.

BARRY: So do I. If the reporters just leave them alone, I'm sure they'll round up the snake who took that child!

Vocabulary Building

Check the glossary for the definitions of these terms:

➤ to bug (v.)

➤ to ferret out (v.)

➤ to hound (v.)

➤ to kidnap (v.)

➤ scared as a rabbit (adj.)

➤ snake (n.)

➤ vulture (n.)

Write a synonym or synonymous phrase for each term in your notebook.

Another Expression

to round up   *to capture*

Questions:

1. What did Barry and Pat learn by watching the news last night?
2. What bugs Barry?
3. According to Pat, what is a reporter's job?
4. What do Barry and Pat think about reporters?
5. Was the little boy's mother happy to be interviewed? How do you know?
6. How does the little boy probably feel?
7. What do Pat and Barry hope will happen?

Role Play

In groups of three, role-play the following situation.

Characters:

AN ACTOR'S WIFE   THE ACTOR'S DAUGHTER   A MAGAZINE REPORTER

Situation:

An 86-year-old actor has just died. As a young man, he was a very popular television and movie star. Many reporters are trying to get information about his recent life and death from his wife and daughter. The wife is willing to talk to a few reporters, but the daughter is upset by all the media attention and doesn't want to talk to any reporters or let her mother talk to them. A reporter who is an old friend of the actor's calls. The wife and daughter must decide what to tell him.

Discussion Topics

Living in the Public Eye: Do you think people who choose to be "in the public eye" (government officials, entertainers, athletes, etc.) have a right to privacy in their personal lives? Why or why not? Give some examples of famous people's personal affairs that you think the public has a right to know about. Give other examples of famous people's personal affairs that should be kept private.

Reporting the News: Describe a reporter's job. Would you like to be a reporter? Why or why not?

The Right to Privacy: Do you think it's appropriate for television news programs, newspapers, and magazines to show pictures of people experiencing grief due to a personal problem or disaster? Why or why not?

Personal Privacy: What does "personal privacy" mean to you? When and where do you want to be alone, if at all? In what situations would you prefer to have no interference whatsoever? Discuss which people you feel have a right to know about your private life and which people do not. Compare and contrast attitudes and practices regarding privacy in various cultures.

The News Story

CHRIS: Did you read the newspaper article about the plane crash in Denver?

PAT: No, I didn't. I know about it though, because I watched the news on TV last night.

CHRIS: Doesn't it make you afraid to fly?

PAT: I've heard that more people die on the road than in the air. Still, I'm a bit chicken about flying.

CHRIS: So am I. I take a rabbit's foot with me and pray at the takeoff and the landing.

PAT: I guess you don't take any chances.

CHRIS: I'm really a coward.

Vocabulary Building

Check the glossary for the definitions of these terms:

➤ to be chicken (v.)

➤ coward (n.)

➤ rabbit's foot (n.)

Write a synonym or synonymous phrase for each term in your notebook.

Questions:

1. How did Chris and Pat learn about the plane crash?
2. Who is afraid to fly?
3. Is driving safer than flying? Why or why not?
4. What brings Chris good luck?
5. What do you do when you are afraid?

Role Play

In groups of three, role-play the following situation.

Characters:

PAT   CHRIS   AN AIRLINE EMPLOYEE

Situation:

Pat and Chris are flying to Los Angeles for a friend's wedding, and they are rushing to catch their plane. They arrived at the airport late because their cab was tied up in traffic. Now they are at the airport and in a hurry to find the correct gate to board the plane. They check the monitor to find their flight number, but they don't see it at all. Did they miss their plane? They ask an airline employee at a nearby counter.

Discussion Topics

Superstitions: What kinds of superstitions do people have in your native country? What are their origins? Are you superstitious? If so, tell about your superstitions. If not, why not?

The News: What are the various sources for obtaining the news? Discuss the pros and cons of each one. Which source do you rely on most? What kind of news interests you the most? What kind of news gives you goose bumps?

Flying: How do you feel about flying? What do you do at the takeoff and at the landing? How often do you fly?

Unit **10**
Politics

Democrats and Republicans

HELEN: What do you think of the presidential choices?

TARA: I don't know much about them.

HELEN: What? Are you an ostrich? Haven't you been watching the party conventions on TV?

TARA: Not really. I've been too busy.

HELEN: The Democratic candidate is short, stocky, and beetle-browed, but the Republican is tall, lanky, and boyish-looking.

TARA: Looks are deceiving. What interests me most is their stands on war and peace. Which one is the hawk?

HELEN: Neither one, really — but the Republican is no dove when it comes to Latin America.

TARA: That's putting your head in the lion's mouth.

HELEN: Does that mean you're for the Democrat?

TARA: Let me learn more about the issues and the candidates' views.

HELEN: OK. That's better than a horseback opinion.

TARA: Right. I promise to ferret out some information, and we'll talk later.

HELEN: Fair enough.

Vocabulary Building

Check the glossary for the definitions of these terms:

➤ beetle-browed (adj.) ➤ horseback opinion (n.)

➤ dove (n.) ➤ ostrich (n.)

➤ to ferret out (v.) ➤ to put one's head in the lion's mouth (v.)

➤ hawk (n.)

Write a synonym or synonymous phrase for each term in your notebook.

Other Expressions

to be for *to support or be in favor of*

Looks are deceiving. *How a person looks has no bearing on how he or she thinks and behaves.*

stand *belief; viewpoint*

Questions

1. What has Helen been watching on TV lately?
2. Why does Helen ask Tara if she is an ostrich?
3. Which presidential candidate is beetle-browed?
4. What interests Tara the most about the presidential candidates?
5. What does Tara want to learn about? Why?
6. What does Helen say about the Republican's stand on Latin America?

Role Play

In groups of five, role-play the following situation.

Characters:

ONE LEGISLATOR FROM EACH OF THESE STATES: NEW YORK, ILLINOIS, CALIFORNIA, COLORADO, AND VERMONT

Situation:

The Legislative Committee on Environmental Protection is meeting to discuss pollution. The members of the committee must decide which kind of pollution should be addressed first with the available government funds. Each legislator speaks for the concerns of his or her home state and the nation as a whole.

Discussion Topics

Party Symbols: The donkey and the elephant symbolize the U.S. Democratic and Republican parties respectively. What is your opinion of these symbols? Do you consider yourself a member of either of these parties? If so, which one? If not, why not?

The President: What is your opinion of the current president of the United States? Would you vote for him if you could? Whom would you like to have for president? What would you like to see the president do?

Equal Rights

MALE CHAUVINIST:	Why are you out on the street campaigning? You should be home cooking for your husband.
FEMINIST:	I'm campaigning for Rita Herrera. The Constitution of the United States guarantees women equal rights, but we won't get them until we have more women in politics.
MALE CHAUVINIST:	Who will take care of the children when all the women are out working?
FEMINIST:	The fathers! The children are theirs, too! Your horse and buggy attitude has seen its day.
MALE CHAUVINIST:	You feminists put a flea in every woman's ear.
FEMINIST:	Thanks a lot. You men are always looking for a scapegoat. If you respected your mothers and wives, there would be no need for our struggle.
MALE CHAUVINIST:	No wonder our society is going to the dogs! When women go to the streets, so do their sons — in gangs.
FEMINIST:	The sins of the fathers are visited upon the sons. Sons model their fathers, not their mothers.
MALE CHAUVINIST:	Well, you'll never convince me.
FEMINIST:	Believe me, I'm not going to waste my time with a male chauvinist pig. I have other fish to fry.

Vocabulary Building

Check the glossary for the definitions of these terms:

- ➤ a flea in one's ear (n.)
- ➤ to go to the dogs (v.)
- ➤ to have other fish to fry (v.)
- ➤ horse and buggy (adj.)
- ➤ male chauvinist pig (n.)
- ➤ scapegoat (n.)

Write a synonym or synonymous phrase for each term in your notebook.

Other Expressions

to have seen its day   *to be out of date; to belong to the past*

The sins of the fathers are visited upon the sons.   *an old saying which means that sons (children) will suffer for their fathers' (parents') sins or wrongdoings*

Questions

1. What is the feminist doing? Why?
2. What does the male chauvinist tell her she should be doing?
3. What reason does the male chauvinist give for his opinion?
4. What does the Constitution of the United States guarantee? Is this guarantee only for women?
5. According to the feminist, what kind of attitude does the male chauvinist have?
6. Why does the male chauvinist say that society is going to the dogs?
7. What does he blame the feminist for doing?
8. How are "the sins of the fathers visited upon the sons"? Give one example.
9. Why can't the feminist and the male chauvinist come to an agreement?

Role Play

In groups of three, role-play the following situation.

Characters:

TWO CANDIDATES FOR GOVERNOR   A TALK SHOW HOST

Situation:

Two candidates for governor are being interviewed on television. The talk show host wants to know how the candidates feel about abortion and state funding for child care. Of course, the candidates must try not to offend future voters. They have opposite opinions on these two issues. Each candidate tries to prove that his or her opinions are the "correct" ones.

Discussion Topics

Feminism vs. Male Chauvinism: Explain the feminist and the male chauvinist points of view as presented in this dialogue. Do you know any "male chauvinist pigs"? Discuss the pros and cons of the feminist and the male chauvinist points of view. What might be a compromise to help in solving the dispute between the sexes?

Equality: Discuss the meaning of equality — ideally and in reality. Have you ever experienced discrimination based on gender, race, ethnic or national origin, religion, handicap, or age? What are some forms or acts of discrimination? Which groups have struggled for equal rights in the United States?

Glossary of Animal-Based Expressions

albatross

Nouns   **albatross**   a heavy weight; something that stifles a person's freedom or peace of mind

animal

Nouns   **animal**   **1.** a person who acts like a beast in terms of manners, cleanliness, or sexual aggressiveness **2.** someone who has a special interest or talent (e.g., city animal)

animal cracker   a cookie or cracker shaped like an animal

animal magnetism   a quality of attraction, charm, or appeal

animal spirits   the vitality that serves as a basis for physical activity and good health

city animal   someone who loves city life

an entirely different animal   something completely different

party animal   someone who loves parties

ant

Verbs   **to have ants in one's pants**   to be nervous or anxious

Adjectives   **antsy**   nervous; restless

ape

Nouns   **ape**   **1.** a person who imitates another **2.** a big, strong man **3.** a hoodlum

Verbs   **to ape** (tr.)   to imitate someone awkwardly; to be a copycat

to go ape over   to become very excited over something or someone

badger

Verbs   **to badger** (tr.)   to pester; to nag at

bat

Nouns   **dingbat**   a stupid person

Verbs   **to bat** (tr.)   to quickly open and close (one's eyes) several times

to have bats in one's belfry   to be crazy

to move/go like a bat out of hell   to move very quickly or suddenly

to not bat an eye   to not show surprise or feelings

Adjectives   **bats, batty**   crazy

bear

Nouns   **bear**   **1.** a person who sells stocks in the belief that prices will go down **2.** a person in a bad mood; a crabby person **3.** a difficult problem **4.** a highway patrol officer

bear hug   the action of one person throwing both arms heartily around another; a big embrace

bearishness   being difficult or disagreeable

Verbs   **to escape the bear and fall to the lion**   to get free of one difficulty but then to get involved in something that is even more complex and dangerous

Adjectives   **bearish**   **1.** rough and gruff like a bear **2.** afraid of or leading to the possibility of prices falling, as in the stock market **3.** having a negative attitude

beast

Nouns   **beast**   an ugly, loathsome person

beastie, beast   a wild or odd person

beastliness   the state of being beastly

beast of burden   **1.** an animal used for carrying heavy objects or for other hard work **2.** a person who is treated like such a beast

the nature of the beast   the essence of a person or thing; the characteristics that are typical of someone or something

Adjectives   **beastly   1.** resembling a beast **2.** unpleasant or disagreeable (e.g., beastly weather)

Adverbs   **beastly**   very (e.g., a beastly hot day)

beaver

Nouns   **beaver**   a hat made of beaver fur or a cloth imitation

eager beaver   a very hyperactive person, especially one who quickly and willingly does assigned tasks

Verbs   **to beaver away** (in.)   to work hard

to work like a beaver   to work extremely hard

Adjectives   **(as) busy as a beaver**   extremely busy

bee

Nouns   **bee**   a get-together for a certain reason (e.g., a quilting bee; a spelling bee)

beehive   1. a crowded area **2.** a women's hairdo that is shaped like a cone or a beehive

Verbs   **to have a bee in one's bonnet**   to have a persistent idea or thought; to have an obsession

to make a beeline (for)   to move quickly and directly toward someone or something

beetle

Adjectives   **beetle-browed**   having bushy eyebrows

bird

Nouns   **bird   1.** an odd person **2.** a woman or girl

birdbrain   a dumb person

the birds and the bees   (knowledge of) sex

a bird's-eye view   a sight observed from a height; an excellent view

gospel bird   a chicken served on Sunday

jailbird   a person who has spent time in jail; an ex-prisoner

Verbs   **to bird-dog** (tr.)   to keep track of; to follow

to eat like a bird   to eat only small amounts; to pick at one's food

to get/give the bird   **1.** to get fired/fire someone from a job **2.** to receive/give a jeer or an insult (often accompanied by a vulgar gesture with the middle finger pointed up and other fingers folded)

to kill two birds with one stone   to solve two problems at the same time; to finish two tasks with a single activity

Adjectives   **birdbrained**   dumb

for the birds (slang)   worthless; undesirable

(as) free as a bird   very free; carefree

Proverbs and Sayings   **A bird in the hand is worth two in the bush.**   Something you already have is better than something more valuable that you only might get.

Birds of a feather flock together.   People of the same type and interests usually prefer each other's company.

The early bird catches/gets the worm.   The person who arrives or gets up early will get the reward.

A little bird told me.   A mysterious or secret person or source provided this information.

buck

Nouns   **buck**   **1.** a one-dollar bill **2.** a young man **3.** obligation

bucktooth   a large front tooth that sticks out

a fast buck   money made without much effort

Verbs   **to buck** (tr.)   to oppose

to buck up (in.) (slang)   to cheer up

to pass the buck   to evade responsibility

Adjectives   **bucktoothed**   having a large front tooth that sticks out

buffalo

Nouns   **buffalo wings**   large, meaty chicken wings, usually deep-fried or barbecued with spices and sauce

Verbs   **to buffalo** (tr.)   to confuse or stump

Adjectives   **buffaloed**   confused, stumped, or stymied

bug

Nouns   **bug**   **1.** a flaw in a computer program **2.** an infection or a germ that causes one **3.** an obsession or an urge **4.** a person who is enthusiastic about something (e.g., a camera bug) **5.** a spy device for listening to other people's conversations

bugbear   a constant source of difficulty

camera bug   a person who is enthusiastic about photography; a shutterbug

firebug   a person who sets illegal, dangerous fires, an arsonist

litterbug   a person who litters in public places

shutterbug   a photography enthusiast; a camera bug

Verbs   **to bug** (tr.)   **1.** to annoy or irritate someone **2.** to conceal a microphone somewhere

to bug out (in.) (slang)   **1.** to pack up and leave **2.** to get out of a place quickly

Adjectives   **bug-eyed**   surprised

(as) cute as a bug's ear   very cute

(as) snug as a bug in a rug   extremely comfortable and content

Proverbs and Sayings   **Bug off!**   Go away!

bull

Nouns   **bull**   **1.** a buyer of securities or commodities who anticipates a rise in price **2.** (slang) a police officer; a private detective or guard **3.** (slang) nonsense

bull in a china shop   a very clumsy person around breakable things; a thoughtless or tactless person

bull pen   **1.** a large prison cell where accused people await their court dates **2.** the place on a baseball field where relief pitchers warm up during a game

bull session   a time of casual conversation or discussion

bull's-eye   the middle of a target

bully   a person who enjoys mistreating weaker people

Verbs   **to bellow like a bull**   to shout with a deep, resonant sound

to bully (tr.)   to treat a person who is younger, weaker, or smaller than oneself with cruelty or force; to overpower someone against his or her will

to seize/take the bull by the horns   to confront a difficult situation bravely

to shoot the bull   to chat and gossip, often without much knowledge of the topics discussed

Adjectives   **bullheaded**   stubborn

bullish   **1.** like a bull **2.** anticipating rising prices (e.g., a bullish market) **3.** thinking positively

Proverbs and Sayings   **Bully for you!**   Good for you!

It's like waving a red flag to a bull.   It's a provocative action or statement, one that might lead to a fight.

bunny

Nouns   **bunny hop**   a dance performed by a line of people hopping and kicking their legs. Each dancer holds onto the waist of the person in front of him or her.

butterfly

Nouns   **butterfly**   **1.** a person who constantly seeks pleasure **2.** a nervous feeling in the stomach, usually caused by tension **3.** a kind of swimming stroke that involves moving both arms in a circular motion and kicking the legs up and down

butterfly chair   a lounge chair made from a metal frame with a canvas cover that is shaped like a pair of wings

butterfly kiss   the action of brushing one's eyelashes against another person's skin

social butterfly   a person who is involved in many activities; one who loves meeting and socializing with people

Verbs   **to butterfly** (tr.)   to split but not completely separate, as with fish or meat

to have/get butterflies in one's stomach   to be or become nervous or agitated

calf

Nouns   **calf   1.** a clumsy, foolish young person **2.** the back part of the lower leg

calf love   a young person's temporary feeling of love

golden calf   a false or unworthy idol (an allusion to the biblical story about people worshiping a calf made of gold instead of worshiping God)

Verbs   **to kill the fatted calf**   to prepare an elaborate banquet in someone's honor (an allusion to the biblical story about the return of the prodigal son)

Adjectives   **calflike**   like a young, clumsy person

camel

Proverbs and Sayings   **That was the straw that broke the camel's back.**   That was the final thing; That was the event that forced a decision or pushed a person to the end of his or her patience.

cat

Nouns   **cat   1.** a fellow; a guy; a dude **2.** a gossipy woman; a sarcastic woman

cat and mouse   the act of teasing someone

catbird seat   a dominant or advantageous position

cat burglar   a lithe and skillful burglar; a thief who enters and leaves a victim's home without detection

catcall   an insulting outcry; a loud call to show anger or disgust at a performance

cat ice   a dangerous situation

cat nap   a short sleep

catnip, catmint   a strong aromatic herb (Nepeta cataria), to which cats are highly attracted

cat's cradle   **1.** a game played by stretching string across a person's fingers to form the shape of a cradle, then transferring the string to someone else's hands to make a different shape **2.** something complicated and intricate

cat's-eye   a semiprecious stone resembling the eye of a cat

catwalk   a narrow path for walking

copycat   someone who mimics or copies the actions of others

fat cat   someone who has great wealth and the accompanying success

pussycat   **1.** a timid male; a softy **2.** a woman or young woman

Verbs   **to bell the cat**   to undertake a hazardous mission; to put oneself in a risky situation

to grin like a Cheshire cat   to smile like the Cheshire cat (the mysterious and broadly smiling cat in *Alice in Wonderland*); to give a large, toothy smile showing pleasure

to lead a cat and dog life   to fight or bicker constantly

to let the cat out of the bag   to reveal a secret or a surprise by accident

to look like the cat that swallowed the canary   to appear successful or extremely happy with oneself; to look smug

to play cat and mouse   to capture and release a person over and over again; to tease or torment

to rain/pour cats and dogs   to rain very hard

to see which way the cat jumps   to wait and see what happens or how a situation is resolved (before making a decision or taking action)

Adjectives   **(as) busy/nervous as a cat on a hot tin roof**   frantically active because of pressure to complete a task

catlike   light on one's feet, like a cat

catty   spiteful; snotty

Proverbs and Sayings   **Cat got your tongue?**   Why are you so quiet? Speak up and answer me!

A cat may look at a king.   Even an inferior has certain rights in the presence of a superior.

Curiosity killed the cat.   It is dangerous to be too curious.

There are more ways than one to skin a cat.   There is more than one way to do something.

There's not enough room to swing a cat.   There's very little space.

When the cat's away, the mice will play.   Whenever a boss or a person in authority is absent, the people in lower positions will enjoy their freedom.

chameleon

Nouns   **chameleon**   **1.** a person or thing that has the ability to change character or form **2.** an untrustworthy person

chick

Nouns   **chick**   a young lady; a girl

chicken

Nouns   **chicken**   **1.** a young or inexperienced person **2.** (slang) a coward

chicken feed   (slang) very little money

chicken scratch   illegible handwriting

spring chicken   a young and possibly naive person

Verbs   **to be chicken**   (slang)   to show fear

to chicken out (in.) (slang)   to withdraw from something due to fear or cowardice

to run around like a chicken with its head cut off   to run around frantically and aimlessly; to be in a chaotic condition

Adjectives   **chickenhearted**   afraid; cowardly

chicken-livered   cowardly

Proverbs and Sayings   **The chickens have come home to roost.**   Justice has been served; a person has received his or her deserved punishment.

Don't count your chickens before/until they're hatched. Don't depend on something that hasn't happened yet.

clam

Nouns   **clam**   **1.** a person who persists in not speaking **2.** a dollar

Verbs   **to be like a clam**   to be quiet and untalkative

to clam up (in.) (slang)   to get quiet or stop talking

Adjectives   **clammy**   cold, wet, and sticky

(as) close/tight as a clam   penny-pinching; stingy

(as) happy as a clam at high tide   very happy

cock

Nouns   **cock**   **1.** a chief person; a leader **2.** a spirited person; a person who has a certain swagger or arrogance

cock-and-bull story   a silly, untrue story; a story that is a lie

cockeye   a half-closed or squinting eye

cock fight   a competition between roosters, usually wearing spurs

cocktail   a cold mixed drink containing alcohol and other ingredients such as seltzer or fruit

weathercock   a person of wavering principles; one who quickly adopts the latest styles and fads

Verbs   **to cock** (tr.)   to move or tilt to one side

Adjectives   **cockamamy, cockamamie**   crazy; ridiculous

cockeyed   **1.** with a half-closed eye; squinty-eyed **2.** a bit crazy **3.** inebriated; drunk

cocksure, cocky   extremely self-confident; overconfident

Proverbs
and Sayings   **Poppycock!**   Nonsense!

coot

Nouns   **coot**   **1.** a person who wouldn't hurt anyone **2.** a fellow

Adjectives   **(as) bald as a coot**   very bald

     (as) crazy as a coot   dotty; senile

cow

Nouns   **cow**   a fat or ugly woman

     coward   a person who lacks courage; a timid, fearful person

     cowardice   fearfulness

     cowboy, cowgirl, cowpoke, cowhand   a person who works on a ranch, usually one who watches the cattle or horses; a person who rides a horse while tending cattle or horses

     cow college   **1.** an agricultural college **2.** an unsophisticated college or university, one without culture or tradition

     cowlick   some strands of hair growing in the direction opposite to the rest of one's hair

     cow town   **1.** a town that is a center for selling or transporting cattle **2.** a small town in a mostly rural area

     sacred cow   a person, thing, or idea that must not be criticized

Verbs   **to cow** (tr.)   to put someone down using threats or displays of power

     to cower (in.)   to show fear, usually by trembling or shrinking back

     to have a cow (slang)   to become very angry or upset

Adjectives   **cowardly**   fearful, lacking courage

Adverbs   **until/till the cows come home**   for a long time

Proverbs
and Sayings   **Don't have a cow!** (slang)   Stay cool and calm; Don't get upset.

     Holy cow!   Wow! (an expression of surprise)

crab

Nouns   **crab**   a person in a bad mood; an unpleasant person

Verbs   **to crab** (in.)   **1.** to complain **2.** to move sideways

Adjectives   **crabbed**   **1.** gloomy; surly **2.** nearly illegible; difficult to understand

crabby   bad-tempered; argumentative; out-of-sorts

crocodile

Nouns   **crocodile tears**   phony, insincere tears

crow

Nouns   **crow's-foot, crow's-feet**   wrinkle(s) near or around the eyes

Verbs   **to crow** (in.)   **1.** to make a noise like a rooster **2.** to express pleasure **3.** to brag or boast

to eat crow   admit an error; to display humility when proved wrong

Adverbs   **as the crow flies**   straight across the land, as opposed to distances measured on a road, river, etc.

cuckoo

Nouns   **cuckoo**   a dumb or silly person

cuckoo clock   a clock with a mechanized cuckoo bird that appears at certain times and makes a cuckoo sound

Verbs   **to cuckoo** (tr.)   to repeat again and again

Adjectives   **cuckoo**   silly; dumb

dog

Nouns   **dog**   **1.** a useless person or thing **2.** an ugly person **3.** a worthless investment

dog and pony show   **1.** a grand sales promotion or publicity demonstration **2.** a speech, skit, or other presentation that is presented frequently

dog days (of summer)   any series of hot, humid days occurring between early July and September in the northern hemisphere

doggie/doggy bag   a bag or container for carrying home one's uneaten food from a restaurant

doggie-do   dog dung or droppings

dog in the manger   a selfish person; one who keeps something that is useless to him or her despite its usefulness to someone else

dogleg   **1.** a sharp turn (as in a road) **2.** something that has a sharp bend or angle

dog meat   a dead person

dog paddle   a simple swimming stroke in which a person paddles and kicks with the arms and legs much like a dog does

a dog's chance   hardly a chance; a very poor chance

a dog's life   a terrible existence

dogwatch   **1.** on a ship, the hours from 4 to 6 and 6 to 8 p.m. **2.** any night shift, especially the last shift

a dog with two tails   someone who is delighted or overjoyed

hair of the dog that bit one   a drink of liquor taken when one is recovering from drinking too much liquor

hot dog   **1.** a sandwich consisting of a long sausage in a bun **2.** a person who shows off

kicking dog   someone who is unjustly blamed; a patsy or scapegoat

sea dog   an experienced or veteran sailor

shaggy-dog story   a long, detailed story about an unimportant event that the storyteller finds humorous but the listener finds boring

tail wagging the dog   a situation in which a small part is controlling the whole thing

three-dog night   a bitterly cold night

top dog   the person in charge or in power

underdog   a person or team that is not expected to win or to succeed in a contest

watchdog   a person who watches over activities to insure their safety or to see that they are done correctly and not wastefully

Verbs   **to bird-dog** (tr.)   to keep track of; to follow

to dog (tr.)   to hound; to go after or follow

to dog it   to not live up to expectations; to shirk one's duties

to dogleg (in.)   to follow a route containing one or more sharp bends

to dog paddle (in.)   to move through water by paddling one's arms and kicking one's legs like a dog

to go to the dogs   to go to ruin; to become worse

to hot dog (it) (in.)   to show off, especially by performing difficult stunts while skiing or surfing

to lead a cat and dog life   to fight or bicker constantly

to look for a dog to kick   to look for someone to blame; to look for a scapegoat

to put on the dog   to dress or entertain in an extravagant or showy manner

to rain/pour cats and dogs   to rain very hard

to see a man about a dog   to leave for some unmentionable purpose (often said for going to the restroom)

Adjectives   **dog-eared**   old and worn out; frayed; having the corners folded down

dog-eat-dog   having hard and cruel competition

dogged   stubborn; unrelenting

dog tired   very tired

hangdog   **1.** guilty **2.** sad, despairing

in the doghouse   in trouble; in someone's disfavor

Adverbs   **doggedly**   stubbornly

Proverbs and Sayings   **Call off the dogs.**   Stop threatening, chasing, or hounding a person.

Doggone it!   an expression of anger or frustration

Every dog has/will have its day.   Everyone will get a chance to be happy and in control.

Let sleeping dogs lie.   One should not search for trouble; One should avoid bringing up things that have happened in the past.

Love me, love my dog.   If you love me, then you must accept my faults along with my good qualities.

You can't teach an old dog new tricks.   Old people can't learn anything new.

donkey

Nouns   **donkey**   the symbol of the Democratic party

dove

Nouns   **dove**   **1.** a woman or child who is gentle **2.** a person who believes in negotiating and compromising to achieve peace; a person who is opposed to war

Verbs   **to dovetail** (tr.)   to join two things for a snug fit; to make into a whole

Adjectives   **dovish**   against war; peaceful

drake

Nouns   **ducks and drakes**   the game of skimming flat stones or shells across the surface of water

Verbs   **to make ducks and drakes of**   to waste; to throw away needlessly or to use recklessly

duck

Nouns   **dead duck**   someone or something doomed to failure or disaster

duck   **1.** a sudden bowing down **2.** a truck that drives on water **3.** a male urinal bedpan **4.** a type of strong, tightly woven cotton fabric

ducks   light clothes made of duck

ducks and drakes   the game of skimming flat stones or shells across the surface of water

duck soup   something very easy to do

duck-squeezer   a person who is strongly concerned about the environment and conservation; an eagle freak

ducktail   a hairstyle that has the hair combed back on both sides so that the two sides come together to make a ridge at the back of the head

lame duck   an elected official who is in office following the election of a successor until the successor's term begins

sitting duck   an easy target for something bad to happen

ugly duckling   someone or something that appears unlikely to succeed but surprisingly turns out well (an allusion to *The Ugly Duckling* by Hans Christian Andersen)

Verbs   **to duck** (in.)   to bend one's body suddenly; to get out of the way

to duck (tr.)   **1.** to push down under water **2.** to lower quickly **3.** to try to escape or avoid

to duck out   to leave quickly and quietly

to duck out of someone/something's way   to move one's body quickly in order to avoid someone or something

to have (all) one's ducks in a row   to have everything in order; to be well organized

to make ducks and drakes of   to waste; to throw away needlessly or to use recklessly

Adjectives   **ducky**   good; fine (often used ironically)

Adverbs   **duckfooted**   with feet pointing outward; with flat feet

like water off a duck's back   easily

like a duck to water   naturally; with enthusiasm

eagle

Nouns   **eagle**   **1.** the symbol and emblem of the United States **2.** one of a pair of silver insignia worn by military colonels and navy captains to show their rank **3.** a ten-dollar U.S. gold coin that has an eagle on the back

eagle eye   1. an exceptional ability to see or observe; also: a person who has this ability **2.** a busybody; a person who monitors other people's actions

eagle freak   someone who has strong concerns about the environment

Verbs   **to spread-eagle** (in.)   to stretch out one's arms and legs like the open wings of an eagle

eel

Verbs   **to hold an eel by the tail**   to struggle to hold onto something slippery; to try to control an impossible situation

Adjectives   **(as) slippery as an eel**   devious; undependable

elephant

Nouns   **elephant**   the symbol of the Republican party

pink elephants   hallucinations caused by overuse of alcohol or certain drugs

white elephant   a useless, unwanted object

Verbs   **to see the elephant**   to do the town; to visit the "big city"; to see the world, especially its bad parts

fawn

Nouns   **fawn**   a beige color, varying from gray to light brown

fawner   a flatterer; a person who pretends to be humble in order to acquire some advantage

Verbs   **to fawn** (in.)   to try to gain favor by flattering or by acting humble and lowly

ferret

Verbs   **to ferret (out)**   to remove or retrieve something with much effort and persistence

fish

Nouns   **cold fish**   a person who is distant and unfeeling

a fine kettle of fish a real mess; an unsatisfactory situation

fish-and-chips a dish of fried fish and french fried potatoes

fish eye a questioning look; an aggressive stare

fishing expedition an investigation that has no definite plan; an exploratory search for facts

fish-or-cut-bait thinking decisive thinking

a fish out of water a person who is uncomfortable due to being in an unfamiliar environment or situation

fish story, fish tale a great big lie; an unbelievable story

neither fish nor fowl not any recognizable or identifiable thing

Verbs **to drink like a fish** to drink (alcoholic beverages) excessively

to feed the fishes to be seasick

to fish (in.) to try to get information from someone in a wily way

to fish for a compliment to try to get someone to pay you a compliment or boost your ego

to fish in troubled waters to take advantage of a bad situation or a person under pressure in order to gain something for oneself

to fish-kiss (in., tr.) to kiss someone with puckered, wet lips

to fish someone or something out **1.** to reach for and reveal **2.** to save someone from drowning

to go fishing for to pull in or draw out of the water as if fishing

to have other fish to fry to have other things to do that are more important

Adjectives **fishy** **1.** dubious, questionable **2.** likely to be improper or illegal

like a fish out of water awkward; uncomfortable

Proverbs and Sayings **All is fish that comes to his/her net.** He or she has the special ability to create successful schemes that make a great deal of money.

Fish or cut bait.   Either do the job you are supposed to do or quit and let someone else do it; Make a decision.

There are plenty of other fish in the sea.   There are many other choices. (used in reference to people, especially those of the opposite sex)

flea

Nouns   **fleabag**   a low-class hotel or rooming house

a flea in one's ear   a bothersome feeling or warning

flea market   a place for buying and selling used items and antiques

flounder

Verbs   **to flounder (around)** (in.)   **1.** to have difficulty moving or standing on one's feet **2.** to proceed uncertainly or ineffectively; to struggle

fly

Nouns   **barfly**   a person who hangs out at a bar; an alcoholic or a frequent drinker

fly   a fishhook disguised with feathers or other ornaments to resemble an insect

fly, fly front   a concealed, usually zippered opening on the front of a pair of pants

a fly in the ointment   a small, unpleasant matter that spoils something; a drawback

fly on the wall   a person who secretly listens to someone else's conversation without being noticed

fly trap   the mouth

gadfly   a pesky person; one who bothers others with crazy schemes

Verbs   **to kill a fly with a bazooka**   to do something in a ridiculously exaggerated or overdone manner

Adjectives   **fly-by-night**   irresponsible; untrustworthy

*Proverbs
and Sayings*   **He wouldn't hurt a fly.** He is completely harmless.

There are no flies on her/him. He or she is a very energetic and active person.

You can catch more flies with honey than with vinegar. You can get what you want more successfully by being pleasant and charming than by being harsh and rude.

fox

Nouns   **fox 1.** a wily, clever person **2.** a good-looking person

foxhole a ditch made by soldiers for protection against enemy fire

fox in a hen house a man who has cleverly arranged to be surrounded by women

fox's sleep a faked sleep; a feigned indifference to what is happening

Verbs   **to outfox** to be smarter (than someone); to outwit

Adjectives   **crazy like a fox** smart and resourceful in spite of appearing to be naive or stupid

foxy 1. shrewd; clever; tricky **2.** good-looking

frog

Nouns   **big frog in a small pond** an important person in the midst of less important people

frog kick in swimming, a kick made with the knees pointing outward

frogman a person who wears a face mask, flippers, and air tank for long periods of underwater swimming

leapfrog a game in which one person bends down while another person jumps over him or her

Verbs   **to have a frog in one's throat** to be hoarse or to sound raspy because of a pain or irritation in the throat

to leapfrog (in.) to go ahead of (each other) in a line; to take turns being in the lead

gander

Nouns   **gander**   a quick look

Verbs   **to take a gander**   to glance; to look at out of curiosity

Proverbs and Sayings   **What's sauce for the goose is sauce for the gander.**   What is appropriate for one is also appropriate for the other. (used especially in male/female comparisons)

goat

Nouns   **goatee**   a small, pointed beard on the chin

scapegoat   a person who is blamed for another person's wrongdoing; someone who is victimized

Verbs   **to get one's goat**   to make someone angry

to play/act the goat   to act recklessly or irresponsibly

to separate the sheep from the goats   to divide people into two groups

goose

Nouns   **cackling geese**   1. people who inform on others 2. people who warn others in order to save, protect, or defend them

goose   a simple-minded person; a silly oaf; a dumb or stupid person

goose bumps, gooseflesh, goose pimples   prickly or bumpy skin caused by fear, excitement, or cold

goose egg   1. a score of zero 2. a bump on the head 3. a failure; a zero

goose step   a lock-kneed step used by some military groups marching on display

wild-goose chase   a worthless search or chase; a waste of time

Verbs   **to cook someone's goose**   to damage or ruin someone; to spoil someone's plans

to go on a wild-goose chase   to waste one's time

to goose (tr.)   to poke one's finger between someone else's buttocks for fun

to goose-step (in.)   **1.** to march with straight legs and locked knees **2.** to thoughtlessly follow convention

to kill the goose that laid the golden egg   to ruin or destroy the source of one's own good fortune

Adjectives   **goosey**   **1.** like a goose **2.** afraid; jumpy **3.** very nervous

(as) loose as a goose   unrestrained

Proverbs and Sayings   **All his/her geese are swans.**   He or she is likely to exaggerate or overestimate.

What's sauce for the goose is sauce for the gander.   What is appropriate for one is also appropriate for the other. (used especially in male/female comparisons)

gopher

Nouns   **gopher**   **1.** an alternate spelling for "gofer," someone who goes for things and brings them back (from "go" + "for") **2.** a dupe; a pawn

gopher ball   a baseball that is pitched in such a way that it is hit for a home run

groundhog

Nouns   **Groundhog Day**   a tradition that takes place on February 2. According to legend, if a groundhog comes out of its hole and sees its shadow (due to a sunny day), there will be six more weeks of winter; but if it's a cloudy day and it doesn't see its shadow, there will be an early spring

grouse

Nouns   **grouse**   a person who complains a lot

Verbs   **to grouse**   to criticize and complain a lot

guinea pig

Nouns   **guinea pig**   **1.** an animal used for research, experimenting, or testing **2.** a scapegoat or patsy; a person manipulated by someone else

hackney

Nouns   **hackney**   a hired car or other vehicle

hackney coach   a horse-drawn coach for hire

Adjectives   **hackneyed**   overused; unoriginal

hare

Nouns   **hare and hounds**   a game in which some players throw pieces of paper to make a trail, and other players try to catch them by following the trail

Verbs   **to run with the hare and hunt with the hounds**   to try to please both sides of a dispute at the same time

Adjectives   **harebrained**   silly; foolish

(as) mad as a March hare   crazy (an allusion to a character in Lewis Carroll's *Alice in Wonderland*)

hawk

Nouns   **hawk**   a person who supports a government policy of war; one with a militant attitude

hawker   a person who sells things

war hawk   a person who favors war

Verbs   **to hawk** (in.)   to make a rasping, throaty sound

to hawk (tr.)   to try to sell something by calling out to potential customers on the street or at a sports stadium

to know a hawk from a handsaw   to realize the difference between two things; to have wisdom

hen

Nouns   **fox in a hen house**   a man who has cleverly arranged to be surrounded by women

mother hen a person whose attitude and actions are very motherly and protective

Adjectives **(as) fussy as a hen with one chick** overly concerned, protective, and picky

henpecked controlled by one's wife

(as) mad as a wet hen extremely angry; outraged

(as) scarce as hen's teeth very rare or nonexistent

herring

Nouns **red herring** something used as a distraction, to draw attention away from a certain issue or truth

hog

Nouns **hog** a selfish or dirty person

hog heaven happiness; an extremely pleasant place or state of being

hog on ice independent in a cocky way; extremely confident

road hog an automobile driver who occupies so much of the road that others cannot pass him or her

Verbs **to go hog-wild** to behave without control or sensible judgment

to go whole hog to do everything possible; to be extravagant

to hog (tr.) **1.** to take more than one deserves; to take more than one's share **2.** to cut the mane of a horse short

to live high off the hog to live in a grand manner, as though one were wealthy

Adjectives **hogtied** **1.** rendered helpless; having the feet tied together at the ankles **2.** married

Proverbs and Sayings **Hogwash!** Not true! Poppycock!

hornet

Verbs **to stir up a hornet's nest** to create trouble or difficulties

horse

Nouns   **charley horse**   a strain or injury that creates pain and stiffness in the (leg) muscles

clotheshorse   a person who loves clothes; one who dresses in a stylish way; a show-off

dark horse   an unknown entrant into a contest; a surprise candidate for political office

horseback opinion   a thoughtless opinion or judgment

horse laugh   a very loud laugh; a mocking, sarcastic laugh

a horse of a different/another color   a completely different thing

horse opera   a Western movie or story

horseplay   roughhousing; wild, physical play

horseplayer   a person who regularly bets on horse races; a gambler

horsepower   a U.S. unit of power equal to 746 watts

horse sense   practical thinking; common sense

horse trade   hard bargaining and negotiating

one-horse town   a small town; a cow town

Trojan horse   a devious trap used to defeat an enemy from within (an allusion to Homer's *Iliad,* in which Greek soldiers hid inside a huge wooden horse that the Trojans took into their city)

war-horse   a veteran soldier or politician

workhorse   **1.** a person who outperforms others; a hard worker **2.** a vehicle or machine that is highly practical and long-lasting

Verbs   **to back the wrong horse**   to make a mistake in judgment; to back a loser

to beat a dead horse   **1.** to continue fighting a battle that has already been won **2.** to keep arguing about a point that has already been settled or that cannot be changed

to change/swap horses in midstream   **1.** to make major changes in an activity that has already begun **2.** to choose someone or something else when it is too late

to get/be on one's high horse   to become or be snobbish or arrogant

to hold one's horses   (slang) to be patient

to horse around (in.)   to play around; to goof around

to horse-trade (in.)   to bargain shrewdly

to not know if one is afoot or on horseback   to be confused; to not know if one is coming or going

to pull in the horses   to get one's things in order

to put the cart before the horse   to have things in the opposite or wrong order; to have things mixed up

to ride a hobby horse   to obsessively pursue a task or scheme

Adjectives   **horse and buggy**   old-fashioned

on one's high horse   snobbish, arrogant

Adverbs   **(straight) from the horse's mouth**   from an authoritative or dependable source

Proverbs and Sayings   **All the king's horses and all the king's men (couldn't put Humpty Dumpty together again.)**   This problem or failed situation apparently can't be resolved or rectified. (an allusion to the Mother Goose rhyme)

Don't look a gift horse in the mouth.   Don't expect perfect gifts; Don't complain about something you haven't paid for.

Hold your horses! (slang)   Wait a minute! Don't be so impatient!

Horsefeathers!   Nonsense! Poppycock!

I'm so hungry, I could eat a horse.   I'm starving.

My kingdom for a horse!   (a quote from Shakespeare's *Richard III*) I'll trade a valuable object for one that is obviously less valuable, but is necessary to me at present.

That's a horse laugh.   That's ridiculous.

You can lead a horse to water, but you can't make him drink.   You can't force someone to do something he or she doesn't want to do.

Wild horses couldn't drag me there. Nothing could force me to go there.

hound

Nouns   **hound**   a person who ceaselessly pursues something (e.g., an autograph hound)

Verbs   **to hound** (tr.)   **1.** to follow persistently, as if with hounds **2.** to harass

Adjectives   **(as) clean as a hound's tooth**   extremely clean

jay

Verbs   **to be naked as a jaybird**   to be entirely naked

to jaywalk (in.)   to cross a street incorrectly or illegally (e.g., to cross against a red light or not at a corner or crosswalk)

jellyfish

Nouns   **jellyfish**   a person without strength of character

Verbs   **to have the backbone of a jellyfish**   to have no backbone

kangaroo

Nouns   **kangaroo court**   **1.** a bogus or extralegal court **2.** a legally convened court operating unjustly

kid

Nouns   **kid**   a child

kid brother, kid sister   younger brother or sister

kidnap(p)er   a person who forcefully takes away another person to gain money or some advantage

whiz kid   a young person with extraordinary intelligence

Verbs   **to treat/handle someone with kid gloves**   to be very careful with a touchy, sensitive, or fearful person

to kid, to be kidding (in., tr.)   **1.** to mock **2.** to fool around **3.** to not be serious

to kidnap (tr.) to unlawfully take someone away, often for the purpose of acquiring a ransom

Proverbs and Sayings **No kidding!** Honestly! Really!

You're kidding! You're joking! You can't be serious!

kitten

Nouns **kitty** a common pot of money in a poker game; a sum of money to be won

Verbs **to feed/fatten the kitty** to add more money to the common pot or winnings while gambling

to have kittens to be angry or excited

Adjectives **kittenish** playful; like a kitten

Adverbs **kitty-corner, kitty-cornered** catercorner; diagonally

lamb

Nouns **lamb** **1.** a sweet and gentle person **2.** a victim; someone easily cheated

Adjectives **(as) innocent as a lamb** naive; guiltless

Adverbs **in two shakes of a lamb's tail** quickly

Verbs **to go in like a lion but come out like a lamb** to go in confidently and aggressively but return humbly

lark

Nouns **lark** a good time; something done just for the fun of it

Adverbs **for a lark** for fun

Verbs **to lark (about)** (in.) to have fun; to do harmless mischief

Proverbs and Sayings **What a lark!** What a joke! How funny!

leech

Nouns **leech** a person who clings to another for free room and board, money, or some other advantage

Verbs   **to leech off (of)** (tr.)   **1.** to suck someone dry **2.** to cling to someone; to live off someone

lion

Nouns   **lion**   an outstanding, remarkable person

the lion's share   the largest portion

Verbs   **to beard the lion in his den**   to face an adversary or enemy on his or her home ground

to go in like a lion but come out like a lamb   to go in confidently and aggressively but return humbly

to lionize (tr.)   to treat something or someone with special regard or significance

to put one's head in the lion's mouth   to look for trouble

Adjectives   **lionhearted**   having a lot of courage

lizard

Nouns   **lounge lizard**   **1.** a man who enjoys pampering women **2.** a parasite on others' good graces

louse

Nouns   **louse**   a loathsome person

Verbs   **to louse up** (in., tr.)   to ruin something; to mess something up

Adjectives   **lousy**   bad or disgusting

magpie

Nouns   **magpie**   **1.** a person who loves to collect anything **2.** a person who talks a lot

mare

Verbs   **to ride shank's mare**   to travel on foot; to walk

mole

Nouns   **mole**   **1.** an undercover agent for the police; a spy **2.** a person who works in darkness

molehill   something small and insignificant

Verbs   **to make a mountain out of a molehill**   to make a major issue out of a minor one; to exaggerate the importance of something

monkey

Nouns   **grease monkey**   a mechanic

monkey   a playful, mischievous, or nimble person

monkey business   silliness; dishonest tricks

monkeyshines   tricks; small acts of mischief

monkey suit   a formal clothing worn by a man; a tuxedo

monkey wrench   something that ruins or destroys

Verbs   **to have a monkey on one's back**   to be addicted to drugs

to monkey (around) (in.)   to behave mischievously

to monkey (around) with (tr.)   to mess or fool around with

Adjectives   **(as) funny as a barrel full of monkeys**   very funny; hilarious

Proverbs and Sayings   **Monkey see, monkey do.**   said of someone who imitates another person or people

moth

Adjectives   **moth-eaten**   **1.** eaten by moths **2.** dog-eared; old and worn out

mouse

Nouns   **cat and mouse**   the act of teasing someone

mouse   **1.** (slang) a woman **2.** a shy person **3.** swollen, darkened skin around the eye caused by being hit; a black eye **4.** a small mobile device used to control the cursor on a computer display

mousetrap   a device that attracts someone for the purpose of capturing or destroying him or her

Verbs **to mickey mouse around** (in.)   to evade any important issue or problem; to waste time; to goof around

to mousetrap (tr.)   to capture with a mousetrap

to play cat and mouse   to capture and release a person over and over again; to tease or torment

Adjectives **mickey mouse**   trivial or unimportant; time-wasting

mousy, mousey   **1.** timid and shy **2.** a grayish brown color

(as) poor as a churchmouse   fine but poor

Proverbs and Sayings **Are you a man or a mouse?**   Are you brave or timid?

When the cat's away, the mice will play.   Whenever a boss or a person in authority is absent, the people in lower positions will enjoy their freedom.

mule

Nouns **mule**   **1.** a very obstinate person **2.** a shoe or slipper that does not have an enclosed back

Adjectives **mulish**   stubborn; obstinate

opossum

Verbs **to play possum**   to pretend to be unaware, asleep, or dead

ostrich

Nouns **ostrich**   a person who tries to stay away from danger or reality by not facing it

Adjectives **ostrichlike**   behaving like an ostrich with its head in the sand; refusing to face reality

owl

Nouns **night owl**   a person who stays out or stays up late at night

oyster

Nouns **oyster**   an extremely disagreeable person

oyster cracker   a small, round, salted cracker

*Proverbs
and Sayings*   **The world is one's oyster.**   One rules the world; One is in charge of everything.

parrot

Nouns   **parrot**   a person who repeats another person's words

Verbs   **to parrot** (tr.)   to repeat without thinking

peacock

Nouns   **peacock**   a person who shows off proudly

Adjectives   **peacockish, peacocky**   showy; proud

pig

Nouns   **little piggy**   the smallest toe on each foot

male chauvinist pig   a man who considers females to be inferior to males

pig   1. a dirty or greedy person 2. (slang) a police officer (used derogatorily)

piggies   toes

piggyback ride   a ride up on another person's shoulders and back

piggy bank   a pig-shaped container used for saving coins

pig latin   a "language" created by systematically changing English

pigs in clover   supposedly rich, genteel people who act unimaginatively

pigskin   a football

pigtail   a braid of hair

Verbs   **to buy a pig in a poke**   to purchase something without first seeing or examining it

to drive one's pigs to market   to snore very loudly

to make a pig of oneself   to eat too much

to pig out (in.) (slang)   to overindulge in food and drink

Adjectives   **piggyback**   **1.** on top of someone's back and shoulders **2.** on a flat railroad car

pigheaded   stubborn

pigeon

Nouns   **clay pigeon**   a gullible person; a sucker

homing pigeon   **1.** a pigeon trained to come back home **2.** a person who always returns home

pigeonhole   a small, open compartment for storing envelopes or other papers

stool pigeon   a person who informs on others; a spy for the police

Verbs   **to pigeonhole** (tr.)   **1.** to put in a hole **2.** to put in a category **3.** to put away

Adjectives   **pigeon-toed**   having toes that turn in

pony

Nouns   **dog and pony show**   **1.** a grand sales promotion or publicity demonstration **2.** a speech, skit, or other presentation that is presented frequently

possum (opossum)

Verbs   **to play possum**   to pretend to be unaware, asleep, or dead

pup, puppy

Nouns   **hush puppies**   small balls of cornmeal dough fried in oil

puppy love   short-term love; an infatuation felt by a young boy or girl

pup tent   a small, two-person tent

rabbit

Nouns   **rabbit ears**   an indoor antenna with two extendable rods that are attached to a base to form a V shape

rabbit food   lettuce; salad greens

rabbit punch   a quick, little punch or hit

rabbit's foot   the separated foot of a rabbit, carried by some people for good luck

Welsh rabbit   melted cheese with spices poured over toast or crackers; Welsh rarebit

Verbs   **to make like a rabbit**   to move fast; to hop to it

to pull a rabbit out of a hat   to achieve an unexpected feat; to find a solution to a seemingly unsolvable or very difficult problem

Adjectives   **(as) scared as a rabbit**   very scared

ram

Verbs   **to ram (into)** (tr.)   to hit something very hard

to ram home an idea   to force something to pass or to be accepted

to ram something down someone's throat   to force something upon someone

rat

Nouns   **pack rat**   a person who likes to collect or keep unnecessary objects

rat   a wretched-acting person; a person who betrays the trust of his or her friends or fellow workers

rathole   a run-down place; a dump

rat race   a dull, repetitive situation; an unrewarding job

Verbs   **to look like a drowned rat**   to be soaking wet

to rat (tr.)   to comb hair in the opposite direction underneath the surface to give the effect of more hair

to rat (on) (tr.) (slang)   to report someone's bad behavior; to tattle on someone

to smell a rat (slang)   to suspect that something is wrong; to sense that someone has caused something to go wrong

*Proverbs
and Sayings*   **They're like rats abandoning a sinking ship.**   They're leaving a person, place, or situation because things have become unpleasant. (a reference to the notion that rats are the first to leave a sinking ship)

raven

Adjectives   **raven**   the glossy black color of a raven

ravenous   extremely hungry and eager for food

robin

Nouns   **round robin**   **1.** a petition or other paper passed around for several people to sign and sometimes add written comments to   **2.** a contest in which every player competes against every other player in turn

rook

Verbs   **to rook** (tr.)   to cheat or swindle

rooster

Nouns   **rooster**   a snobbish, conceited person

rooster tail   a tall, vertical spray of water shooting out from a fast-moving motorboat

shark

Nouns   **card shark**   a person who is an expert card player

shark   **1.** a dangerously tricky person who victimizes others by extorting or lending money   **2.** a person who is extremely successful due to his or her abilities in a particular field

sheep

Nouns   **black sheep**   **1.** a person who is the worst member of a family or group; one who is the cause of embarrassment for others   **2.** a strange person; an oddball; a person who doesn't fit in with the rest of the group

sheep **1.** a timid, mild, or vulnerable creature **2.** a person who can be easily influenced

sheepskin a diploma or degree

Verbs **to make sheep's eyes (at someone)** to look lovingly or desiringly at someone

to separate the sheep from the goats to divide people into two groups

Adjectives **sheepish** **1.** like a sheep in passiveness, shyness, or stupidity **2.** showing embarrassment

shrew

Nouns **shrew** a bad-tempered, complaining woman

Adjectives **shrewish** bad-natured; crabby and disagreeable

skunk

Nouns **skunk** a badly behaved person; a rat

Verbs **to get skunked** (in.) to become drunk

to skunk (tr.) **1.** to defeat; to shut out of a game **2.** to not pay; to cheat

Adjectives **(as) drunk as a skunk** quite drunk; inebriated

sloth

Nouns **sloth** **1.** an extremely lazy person **2.** lack of interest and/or willingness to do things

Adjectives **slothful** lazy

snail

Nouns **snail** a person or thing that moves very slowly

Adjectives **snail-paced** very slow-moving

Adverbs **at a snail's pace** very slowly

snake

Nouns **snake** a person who has little worth and no scruples

snake charmer a person who entertains other people with his or her power to charm or fascinate poisonous snakes; a person who uses charm to gain advantage

snake dance **1.** a dance in imitation of snakes, or one in which snakes are used or honored **2.** in a celebration or ceremony, a dance performed by a group of people who move along in a line

snake eyes the two in dice, one spot on each die

snake-in-the-grass **1.** a disloyal, secretive friend **2.** a sneaky, despised person

snake oil **1.** a mixture or substance that is sold as medicine but has no proven medicinal value; phony or bogus medicine **2.** bull, balderdash

snake pit **1.** an institution for the mentally ill **2.** a place of chaos and confusion

Verbs **to nourish a snake in one's bosom** to be kind to a person who does not appreciate it or who acts like a snake

to snake (in.) to move like a snake; to move secretively

to snake (tr.) **1.** to move something by dragging it along or by pulling it **2.** to move as a snake moves

sow

Verbs **to make a silk purse out of a sow's ear** to create something of value out of something of no value (often used in the negative)

spider

Nouns **pink spiders** pink elephants; hallucinations caused by overuse of alcohol or certain drugs

spider veins varicose veins located just below the surface of the skin

Adjectives **spidery** like a spider or a spiderweb

sponge

Nouns   **sponge**   **1.** a person who lives off of others; a sponger **2.** yeast dough that has been raised **3.** a dessert containing whipped egg whites or gelatin

sponger   a person who lives by means of financial assistance from others

Verbs   **to sponge** (tr.)   **1.** to clean with a sponge **2.** to absorb

to sponge on (tr.)   to leech off; to live off of; to take advantage of

Adjectives   **spongy**   like a sponge; soft and full of holes; absorbent

squirrel

Nouns   **squirrel**   **1.** a strange or eccentric person **2.** a car engine's horsepower

Verbs   **to squirrel away** (tr.)   to put away for safekeeping; to hide

Adjectives   **squirrelly**   crazy; nutty

steer

Verbs   **to steer clear of**   to keep away from; to avoid

stork

Nouns   **a visit from the stork**   the birth of a baby

Verbs   **to expect the stork**   to expect or to wait for the birth of a baby

swan

Nouns   **swan song**   the final work of a poet, writer, or other artist; the final appearance of a performer

Proverbs and Sayings   **All his/her geese are swans.**   He or she is likely to exaggerate or overestimate.

swine

Nouns   **swine**   a horrible, loathsome person

Verbs   **to cast (one's) pearls before swine**   to waste something good on someone who doesn't care about it

tiger

Nouns   **paper tiger**   someone or something that is not as dangerous or tough as it appears

tiger   **1.** a dangerous and wild person **2.** an energetically aggressive person

tigereye, tiger's-eye   a semiprecious yellowish stone (silicified crocidolite)

Verbs   **to have a tiger by the tail**   to have become associated with something powerful and potentially dangerous

to ride the tiger   to prevail despite great difficulty

toad

Nouns   **toad**   a disgusting person or thing

toady   a person who flatters another in order to gain some advantage; a fawner

Verbs   **to toady**   to flatter for some selfish purpose; to fawn

tortoise

Nouns   **tortoise**   something or someone considered to be slow-moving or lazy

turkey

Nouns   **jive turkey**   a stupid person

turkey   **1.** an idiotic person; one without any talent **2.** a failure or flop; especially a show, play, or movie that has failed

Verbs   **to stop/quit/go cold turkey**   to stop suddenly and completely, without tapering off

to talk turkey   **1.** to speak frankly **2.** to talk business

Adverbs   **cold turkey**   suddenly and completely, without tapering off

turtle

Nouns   **turtleneck**   **1.** a round, high, close-fitting collar that can be easily turned down **2.** a sweater that has such a neck

Verbs   **to turn turtle**   to turn upside down or flip over; to capsize

vulture

Nouns   **vulture**   an overly greedy person; one who preys on or stalks others

wasp

Nouns   **WASP**   an acronym for White Anglo-Saxon Protestant, the Caucasian and Protestant power group in the United States; a member of the dominant, privileged class in the U.S., often used negatively

wasp waist   a small, thin waist

Adjectives   **Waspish, Waspy**   having the qualities of the dominant class in the U.S.

waspish   **1.** sharp-tongued **2.** small in build

weasel

Nouns   **weasel**   a sneaky person

weasel word   an evasive word

Verbs   **to weasel** (in.)   to use evasive language; to be indirect

to weasel out of   to get out of doing something, especially some responsibility

whale

Nouns   **whale**   a large or fat person

Verbs   **a whale of a difference**   a tremendous difference

to have a whale of a time   to enjoy oneself greatly; to have an exciting time

to whale (tr.)   **1.** to defeat **2.** to hit energetically and hard

to whale the tar out of   to beat up; to hit repeatedly

wolf

Nouns **lone wolf** a man who stays to himself; a loner

wolf **1.** a Romeo; a Don Juan; a man who aggressively pursues women for their affections **2.** a person who is vicious, greedy, and destructive

wolf in sheep's clothing a threatening or dangerous person or thing disguised as something gentle and mild

wolf whistle a special kind of whistle a person makes to show admiration or sexual desire for a person of the opposite sex

Verbs **to cry wolf** to cry or complain about something when nothing is really wrong

to hold a wolf by the ears **1.** to place oneself in jeopardy **2.** to be in a dilemma

to keep the wolves/wolf from the door to maintain oneself at a minimal level; to keep from starving, freezing, etc.

to throw someone to the wolves to sacrifice someone; to offer another person to harm in order to save oneself or to serve one's own interests

to watch out for the wolves to beware of people who will harm you or take advantage of you

to wolf (down) (tr.) to gobble something up; to eat something quickly and greedily

Adverbs **like a wolf in the fold** slyly and unexpectedly

worm

Nouns **bookworm** a person who spends most of his or her time reading

a can of worms **1.** a mess **2.** a sensitive subject

worm **1.** a contemptible person **2.** a pitiful person

Verbs **to open (up) a can of worms** to uncover a set of problems

to worm (one's way) (in.) to move sneakily

to worm one's way into   to sneakily include oneself in other people's conversation or introduce oneself without being invited to do so

to worm one's way out of   to squeeze or wiggle out of a problem or responsibility

to worm something out of someone   to convince someone to give you something

Proverbs
and Sayings   **The early bird catches/gets the worm.**   The person who arrives or gets up early will get the reward.

Idioms and Other Expressions

to bail someone out   to get someone out of trouble

to be born yesterday   to be inexperienced or naive

to be caught in a bind   to be in a difficult situation

to be finished   to be dead

to be for   to support or be in favor of

to be in for a surprise   to be due for a surprise

to be in for ten years   to have ten years to serve in confinement or in prison

to be made up   to be wearing a lot of makeup or cosmetics

to be on for   to be responsible for; to be the one to do something

to blow an amount of money   to spend or waste that amount of money

bound for   on the way to; planning to go to

to bring something up   to mention something

to burrow   to dig into

can't stand   can't tolerate

to carry on   to behave in a foolish, excited, or improper manner

to change one's mind   to change one's opinion or decision

close call   narrow escape

Come along.   Come with me.

come to think of it   on second thought; when I reflect on it

con artist   someone who makes a living by swindling people

cool dude   a very clever, controlled person

to cover for someone   to protect someone (who might get into trouble) by making an excuse or telling a lie

Crime doesn't pay.   Crime will not benefit a person.

to cut a class   to be absent from a class

Don't be cute.   Don't try to be clever.

to do someone a favor   to do something nice for someone

down in the mouth   sad-faced; unsmiling

to drive someone crazy   to annoy or disturb someone

Easy come, easy go.   When you get something easily, you may lose it just as easily.

econ   an abbreviation for *economics*

to fix someone up   to make a match; to bring together two people who might become romantically involved

from now on   starting today and lasting forever

gem   a valuable or good person

to get one's act together   to get organized; to be in control

to get on one's nerves   to irritate or bother a person

to get the most out of something   to take advantage of something to the fullest; to capitalize on something

to give up on someone   to forget about or abandon someone

Go for it!   Do it! Try your best! Grab the opportunity!

to go with   to match in color and style

to have a heart   to be kind and generous

to have a lot going for one   to have many advantages

to have connections   to have friends in important positions

to have seen its day   to be out of date; to belong to the past

to have time off   to be free, especially to be free from work

health food   food that is believed to promote good health

Hold on a minute!   Wait! Be patient!

to hop to it   to move quickly in a certain direction

how come   why

How dumb can you get!   someone (either the speaker, the listener, or a third person) has done something very dumb

I beg your pardon?   Excuse me. (used with rising intonation if the listener is confused)

If you don't like the weather today, wait until tomorrow.   The weather is very changeable.

in Dutch   in trouble

to introduce someone around   to introduce someone to several other people, especially at a party or a group meeting

It's not the end of the world.   It's not all that bad; this one event won't ruin your whole life.

It's your funeral!   If you do it, you will suffer all the consequences.

to kowtow   to defer to; to fawn over

to lead someone on   to falsely encourage a person's affections

to learn one's lesson   to learn something from experience; to learn something the hard way

to learn something the hard way   to learn something from an unpleasant experience

lined up   planned or arranged

lit   an abbreviation for *literature*

to live to regret something   to suffer the consequences of one's actions

to look after   to watch; to take care of

to look as if one has lost one's best friend   to look very sad and depressed

Looks are deceiving.   How a person looks has no bearing on how he or she thinks and behaves.

to loosen up   to become relaxed

to lose one's nerve   to lose confidence; to get scared

to make a killing   to be successful by making a lot of money

to make heads or tails out of   to understand

to make it   to come; to attend something

to make sense   to be understandable

makeup   the opportunity given by a teacher to do an assignment or take a test at a later time

mean dancer   a very good dancer

to mind   to dislike; to be against

to move out   to take one's belongings and leave a living or working place

neat   great; excellent

not for the world   not for anything (no matter what its value)

Nothing ventured, nothing gained.   If you don't try to do something, you will never achieve it or profit from it.

No way!   Absolutely not.

no wonder   not surprising

on one's mind   occupying one's thoughts

on second thought   after thinking it over

on the other hand   from another point of view

on top of that   in addition to that

open   straightforward; honest

to pass on something   to refuse something

to pay through the nose   to pay too much

to play the market   to participate in trading; to invest in stocks and bonds

potluck   a party (usually a dinner) to which each guest brings something to eat or drink

to pull out   to quit

to pull the wool over someone's eyes   to try to fool someone

pushy   overly bold

to put up a good front   to show your best characteristics; to act brave and confident

to put up with   to tolerate

to round up   to capture

to run an errand   to take a short trip to do a specific thing

rundown   an item-by-item report; a summary

to shake   to get rid of

sharp   fashionable or attractive

to show someone the ropes   to share one's knowledge and experience with someone else

shrink   a psychoanalyst or psychotherapist

The sins of the fathers are visited upon the sons.   an old saying which means that sons (children) will suffer for their fathers' (parents') sins or wrongdoings

to skate on thin ice   to be in a risky situation

stand   belief; viewpoint

the star student   the best student

to stick something out   to endure something

to stick up for   to support

to stick with   **1.** to stay with; to stay close to **2.** to have; to remain with

to take someone under one's wing   to protect and guide someone

to take something   to tolerate or endure something

tattletale   one who tells other people's secrets

to tick someone off   to make someone angry

traffic jam   such heavy traffic that the cars can't move

to turn out right   to end satisfactorily

to turn up   to appear

two-timer   a person who deceives a boyfriend or girlfriend by secretly going out with another person for romantic reasons

What's up?   What is happening?

Where do I come in?   What do you want me to do?

You bet.   Yes, I agree.

You can't win them all.   It's not possible to win at everything you do. You can't always be right.

You've got me there.   I admit you're right about that.

About the Author

Grete Roland has extensive experience in both language learning and language teaching. She taught EFL in Norway, Germany, and Turkey for four years and has taught ESL in the United States for over twenty years. She also has taught English, speech, and education courses. Presently at National-Louis University's National College of Education she holds the positions of Director of Graduate Programs for the Chicago Campus; ESL and Bilingual Coordinator for three campuses; and Assistant Professor in Curriculum and Instruction for the ESL and bilingual program concentration. She holds a Ph.D. in comparative-international education and M.S. degrees in linguistics and in multicultural education.